DO NOT (APPREHEND)

DANGER

IGORATION
INCHORATE

DON inevitable

IN GREEN PASTURES

IN GREEN PASTURES

DAILY READINGS FOR
EVERY DAY IN THE YEAR

By

J. R. MILLER, D.D.

Author of 'Come Ye Apart' etc.

ISBN 1-84550-032-6

© Christian Focus Publications 2005

10 9 8 7 6 5 4 3 2 1

Reprinted in 2005
in the
Christian Heritage Imprint
by
Christian Focus Publications
Geanies House, Fearn, Tain, Ross-shire,
IV20 1TW, Great Britain

www.christianfocus.com

Cover design by Alister MacInnes

Printed and bound by
Bercker, Germany

Contents

These readings
have been selected and arranged
by
Mary A. Butler

JANUARY

January 1

'THE LORD WILL PROVIDE'

Write deep in your heart this New Year's day this word of sublime confidence, JEHOVAH-JIREH. It tells you that you can trust God always; that no promise of his ever fails; that he doeth all things well; that out of all seeming loss and destruction of human hopes he brings blessing. You have not passed this way heretofore. There will be sorrows and joys, failures and successes, this year, just as there were last year. You cannot forecast individual experiences. You cannot see a step before your feet. Yet Jehovah-jireh calls you to enter the new year with calm trust. It bids you put away all anxieties and forebodings – 'The Lord will provide.'

CHRIST OUR BIOGRAPHER

We need not trouble to keep diaries of our good deeds or sacrifices, or to write autobiographies with pages of record for the things we have done. We may safely let our life write its own record, or let Christ be our biographer. He will never forget anything we do, and the judgment day will reveal everything. The lowliest services and the obscurest deeds will then be manifested.

January 2

TRUE LIVING

Life means far more than many of us ever dream of. It is not merely passing through the world with a fair measure of comforts, with enough bread for our hunger, with enough raiment to keep us warm. Life means growth into the image of Christ himself, into strength, into well-rounded character, into disciplined manhood and womanhood, into the blessed peace of God. But all the peace into which he guides us is victory over all the trials, a quietness and confidence which no external circumstances can break.

January 3

SCRIPTURE TRUTH

Character never can be strong, noble, and beautiful, nor can conduct be worthy of intelligent beings bearing God's image, if Scripture truth be not wrought into the very soul by personal search and pondering. Let us not stay for ever in the primer of religious knowledge, amid the easy things that we learned at our mother's knee. There are glorious things beyond these; let us go on to learn them. The word of Christ can get into your heart to dwell in you and transform you only through intelligent thought and pondering.

January 4

FINDING OUR MISSION

We need never be anxious about our mission. We need never perplex ourselves in the least in trying to know what God wants us to do, what place he wants us to fill. Our whole duty is to do well the work of the present hour. There are some people who waste entire years wondering what God would have them do, and expecting to have their life-work pointed out to them. But that is not the divine way. If you want to know God's plan for you, do God's will each day; that is God's plan for you today. If he has a wider sphere, a larger place for you, he will bring you to it at the right time, and then *that* will be God's plan for you and your mission.

> Our lives we cut on a curious plan,
> Shaping them, as it were, for man;
> But God, with better art than we,
> Shapes them for eternity.

January 5

PRAYER IN BUSY DAYS

It is in prayer that God shows his face to his children, that they have visions of his beauty and glory, that the sweet things of his love come down as gifts into their hearts, and that they are transformed into his likeness. If you would be blessed, get many seasons of prayer into your busy, harassed, tempted, struggling life. It is in these quiet moments that you really grow. Somewhere in every vexed, feverish day get a little 'silent time' for prayer. It will bring heaven down into your heart and make you strong for service.

January 6

SYMPATHY OF CHRIST

Unless words mean nothing, unless the Scriptures cheat us with poetical images and illusions, Christ feels our every grief and every struggle, and sympathizes with us in each one. Remember how his heart responded when he was on earth to all human need. Sorrow stirred his compassion. Every cry of distress went to the depths of his soul. That heart is still the same. When angels are thronging about him, and a poor weary sufferer in some lowly home on earth, or a stricken penitent crouching in some darkness, reaches out a trembling finger-tip of faith and touches the hem of his garment, he turns about with loving look and asks, 'Who touched me?'

January 7

YES AND NO

There is tremendous power in the little monosyllable 'No' when it is spoken resolutely and courageously. It has often been like a giant rock by the sea as it has encountered and hurled back the mighty waves of temptation. It is a majestic power the power to say 'No' to everything that is not right. But it is just as important to learn to say 'Yes'. There comes to us offers and solicitations we must not reject, and opportunities we must not throw away. Life is not all resistance and defence. Whatever is wrong we must meet with a firm, strong, uncompromising 'No'; but whatever is right we should welcome into our life with a hearty, cheerful 'Yes'.

January 8

DISCIPLINE OF DRUDGERY

There is nothing like life's drudgery to make men and women of us. You chafe under it. You sigh for leisure, to be freed from bondage to hours to duties, to tasks, to appointments, to rules, to the treadmill round. Yet this is God's school for you. It may be a cross. Yes; but all true blessing comes to us hidden under the ruggedness and the heaviness of a cross. We do not grow most in the easiest life. Accept your treadmill round, your plodding, your dull task-work, and do all well – do always your best – and you will grow into strong, noble character.

January 9

GOD'S GIVING

God does not dole out help by little grains. He pours out blessings until there is no more room to receive. He gives until our emptiness is altogether filled. He is never done giving when you cease receiving – he could give far more. Nothing limits the supplies we get from God save our capacity to take. He would give infinitely if we had room to receive infinitely, and the only reason we are not supplied in this glorious way, according to God's riches, is because we will not take all that God would give. The only thing that stands in the way of our being blessed to the full is the smallness of our faith.

January 10

OUR CLUMSY HANDS

Most of us are awkward in doing even our most loving deeds. We must learn to be patient, therefore, with people's awkwardness and clumsiness. Their hearts may be gentler than their hands. Do not misinterpret their actions, finding enmity where purest love is, indifference where affection is warmest, slights where honour was meant. Away with your petty suspicions! Be patient even with people's faults. Let us train ourselves to find the best we can in every act of others, to believe the best always of people and their actions, and to find some beauty in everything.

January 11

GOD'S BETTER ANSWER

God many times answers our prayers not by bringing down his will to ours, but by lifting us up to himself. We grow strong, so as to need no longer to cry for relief. We can bear the heavy load without asking to have it lightened. We can keep the sorrow now and endure it. We can go on in quiet peace without the new blessing which we thought so necessary. We have not been saved from the battle we shrank so from entering, but we have fought it through and have gained the victory. Is not victoriousness in conflict better than being freed from the conflict? Is not peace in the midst of the storm and the strife better than to be lifted altogether over the strife?

January 12

TOUCHING OTHERS

There are some good people who seem to want to be your friends and to do you good, but they stay at a distance, and never come near you. Then there are others who draw close to you, and look into your eyes and touch you with their hands. You know the difference between these two ways of helping. The former persons give you only cold help, with no part of themselves, no tender sympathy; the latter may give you really less of material help, but they pour a portion of their own warm life into your soul. Christ never withheld his touch; he always gave part of himself. We should be the touch of Christ to others. His love should tingle in our very fingers when they touch others.

January 13

FIDELITY TO DUTY

Too often we want to know how duty is going to come out before we are ready to accept it and do it. But that is wrong, for we have nothing whatever to do with the cost or with the outcome of duty; we have to know only that it is duty, and then go right on and do it. The true way to live is to bring to each duty that comes to our hand our wisest thought and our best skill, doing what appears to us at the time to be the right thing to do, and then leaving it, never regretting nor fretting about results. God has promised to guide us, and if we are living in true relations to him, we may expect guidance moment by moment as we go on.

January 14

HAVING – GIVING

It is not having that makes men great. A man may have the largest abundance of God's gifts – of money, of mental acquirements, of power, of heart-possessions and qualities – yet if he only holds and hoards what he has for himself, he is not great. Men are great only in the measure in which they use what they have to bless others. We are God's stewards, and the gifts that come to us are his, not ours, and are to be used for him as he would use them. When we come to Christ's feet in consecration, we lay all we have before him. He accepts our gifts; and then putting them back into our hands, he says, 'Go now and use them in my name among the people.'

January 15

AN EYE FOR MOTES

We ought not to expend all our keen-sightedness in discovering our neighbour's little faults. By some strange perverseness in human nature, we have far keener eyes for flaws and blemishes in others than for the lovely things that are in them. Not many of us go about talking to every one we meet about our neighbour's good points, and praising the lovely things in him. Not a few of us, however, can tell of an indefinite number of faults in many of our neighbours. Would it not be well to change this, and begin gossiping about the good and beautiful things in others?

January 16

SILENCE THAT IS NOT GOLDEN

Is any miserliness so mean as that which holds loving and gentle words in the heart unspoken when dear lives are starving close beside us which our words would save and feed? Use your gift of speech to give comfort, joy, cheer, and hope to all about you. Use it to encourage the weary and disheartened, to warn those who are treading in paths of danger, to inspire the lethargic and indolent with high and holy motives, to kindle the fires of heavenly aspiration on cold heart-altars.

January 17

CHRIST IN US

We should not be satisfied with any small measures of attainment. If Christ dwells in each Christian, we should all be new incarnations. Christ himself was the incarnation of God. He said, 'He that hath seen me hath seen the Father.' If we are Christians, we are new incarnations of Christ. We should be able to say to men: 'Look at me, and see what Christ is like.' The beauties of Christ should be seen in us. This will become true just in the measure in which the Christ in us is allowed to rule us and transform our lives. It should be our aim and prayer that the divine abiding in us may be without hindrance, and that no part of our life shall remain unfilled.

January 18

PRACTICAL KINDNESS

Kindness must be practical, not merely emotional and sentimental. It should not be satisfied with good wishes, sympathetic words, or even with prayers; it should put itself into some form that will do good. There are times when even prayer is a mockery. It is sometimes our duty to answer our own requests, to be ourselves the messengers we ask God to send to help others. We are God's angels when we find ourselves in the presence of human needs and sorrows which we can supply or comfort. Expressions of pity or sympathy are mockeries when we try to do nothing to relieve the distress.

January 19

BEING – DOING

There is a silent personal influence, like a shadow, that goes out from every one, and this influence is always leaving results and impressions wherever it touches. You cannot live a day and not touch some other life. Wherever you go your shadow falls on others, and they are either better or worse for your presence. Our influence depends upon what we *are* more than upon what we do. It is by living a beautiful life that we bless the world. I do not underestimate holy activities. Good deeds must characterize every true life. Our hands must do mighty works. But if the life itself is noble, beautiful, holy, Christ-like, one that is itself a benediction, an inspiration, the worth of the influence is many times multiplied.

January 20

PREACHING BY SHINING

There is not a Christian who cannot preach sermons every day, at home and among neighbours and friends, by the beauty of holiness in his own common life. Wherever a true Christian goes his life ought to be an inspiration. Our silent influence ought to touch other lives with blessing. People ought to feel stronger, happier, more earnest after meeting us. Our very faces ought to shed light, shining like holy lamps into sad and weary hearts. Our lives ought to be benedictions to human sorrow and need all about us.

January 21

TOO LATE AFTER-THOUGHTS

There is a time for the doing of the duties which are assigned to us. If we will do them in their own time, there will be a blessing in them. If, however, we do not perform them at the right moment, we need scarcely trouble ourselves to do them at all. The time to show interest and affection to any sufferer is while the suffering is being endured, not next day, when it is all over, when the person is well again or – dead. Oh, there are so many of us whose best and truest thoughts are always after-thoughts, too late to be of any use! We see when all is over what noble things we might have done if we had only thought.

January 22

SERVING IN LOVE

Work in Christ's vineyard, gifts to missions, charities dispensed to the poor, money given to good causes, ministries among the sick and the needy – these things please Christ only when there is in them all love for him, when they are done truly for him, in his name. We need to look honestly into our hearts while we crowd our days with Christian activity, to know what the spirit is which prompts it all. 'Lovest thou *me*?' is the Master's question as each piece of service is rendered, as each piece of work is done. There is no other true motive.

January 23

THE HIDING AWAY OF SELF

No grace shines more brightly in a Christian than humility. Wherever self comes in it mars the beauty of the work we are doing. Seek to do your work noiselessly. Do not try to draw attention to yourself, to make men know that *you* did this beautiful thing. Be content to pour your rich life into other wasted, weary lives, and see them blessed and made more beautiful, and then hide away and let Christ have the honour. Work for God's eye, and even then do not think much about reward. Seek to be a blessing, and never think of self-advancement. Do not worry about credit for your work or about monuments; be content to do good in Christ's name.

January 24

'NOT AS I WILL'

We pray earnestly, pressing our very heart into the heavens, but it is for the doing of our own will that we ask, not for the doing of God's will. Is it the true child-spirit for us to insist on having our way with God, to press our will without regard to his? Are we not God's children? Is it not ours to learn obedience and submission in all things to him? No prayer is acceptable to God which, after all its intensity and importunity, is not still referred to God and left to his superior wisdom. Who but he knows what is best for us?

January 25

SPIRITUAL GREATNESS

Spiritual greatness – sanctified character, beauty of soul, the likeness of God upon the life, heart-qualities – shall endure for ever. Into this true spiritual greatness God wants to train every one of us. Many Christians grow sadly disheartened because they seem never to become any better. Year after year the struggle goes on with the old tempers and ugly dispositions, the old selfishness, pride, and hatefulness, and they appear never to be growing victorious. Yet Christ is a most patient teacher. He never wearies of our slowness and dulness as scholars. He will teach the same lesson over and over until we have learned it. If we only persevere, he will never tire of us, and his gentleness will make us great.

January 26

PATIENT LOVE

'As I have loved you' means love that is sweet, fragrant and gentle to men who have many rudenesses and meannesses, who are selfish and faulty, with sharp corners and but partially sanctified lives and very vexing ways. If all Christian people were angelic, and you were too, it would not be hard to love all; but as many other people are not yet angelic, you will still have need of patience, even if you are angelic yourself – which probably you are not.

January 27

CONTROL OF TEMPER

The worst-tempered people may be made gentle and loving in all speech, act and disposition by the renewing and transforming power of diviner grace. God can take the jangled keys and put them in tune if we will but put them into his hand. But we must strive ourselves to be sweet-tempered. We must watch the rising anger and quickly choke it back. We must keep down the ugly dispositions. We must learn to control ourselves, our tempers, our feelings, our passions, our tongues. We must seek to develop the gentle things and crowd out the nettles. The discipline is not easy, but the lesson can be mastered.

January 28

'AS WE FORGIVE'

In the model prayer which Christ gave to his disciples he linked together the divine and the human forgiveness. While we pray to God to forgive our countless and enormous sins, we are taught to extend to others who harm us in little ways the same forgiveness which we ask for ourselves. Let us keep no bitterness in our hearts for a moment. Let us put away all grudges and all ill-feelings. Let us remember the good things others do to us and forget the evil things. Then we can pray sincerely, 'Forgive us as we forgive.' If we cannot do this, I do not know how we are going to pray at all for forgiveness.

January 29

THE TEST OF LOVE

There is a great difference between love for people you never saw and never shall see and for those with whom you mingle in close relations. There are some persons who souls glow with compassionate affection for the Chinese, the Hindus, the Japanese, who yet utterly fail in loving their nearest neighbours, those who jostle against them every day in business, in pew, in church-aisle, in society. The test of Christian love is that it does not fail even when brought into closest contact, into the severest frictions, of actual living.

January 30

WINNING SOULS

We must love those we seek to save, but we must love Christ more; we must love them because we love Christ, because he loves them, because he gave himself for them. We must strive to win souls, not for ourselves, but for Christ. It is not enough to get people to love us; we must get them to love our Saviour, to trust in him, and to commit their lives to him. We must hide ourselves away out of sight. He who is thinking of his own honour as he engages in any Christian service is not a vessel ready to be used by Christ. We need to take care that no shadows of ourselves, of our pride, our ambition, our self-seeking, fall upon our work for Christ.

January 31

BLESSINGS OF TRIBULATION

When you have passed through a season of suffering and stand beyond it, there ought to be a new light in your eye, a new glow in your face, a new gentleness in your touch, a new sweetness in your voice, a new hope in your heart, and a new consecration in your life. You ought not to stay in the shadows of the sorrow, but to come again out of them, radiant with the light of victory and peace, into the place of service and duty. The comfort that God gives puts deep new joy into the heart, and anoints the mourner or the sufferer with a new baptism of love and power.

FEBRUARY

February 1

CONTENTMENT, NOT SATISFACTION

We must distinguish between contentment and satisfaction. We are to strive to be content in any state; we are never to be satisfied in this world, whether our circumstances are prosperous or adverse. Satisfaction can come only when we awake in Christ's likeness in the world of eternal blessedness. We are not to seek contentment by restraining or crushing the infinite cravings and longings of our souls. Yet we are meant as Christians to live amid all circumstances in quiet calmness and unbroken peace, in sweet restfulness of soul, wholly independent of the strifes and storms about us, and undisturbed by them. Content in whatever state, yet never satisfied – that is the ideal life for every Christian.

February 2

SERVING CHRIST AT HOME

Many people think that work for Christ must be something outside, something great or public. They imagine that to minister to Christ they must teach a Sunday-school class or join a missionary society, or go out to visit sick people, or go into hospitals or prisons on missions of mercy. These are all beautiful and important ministries, and Christ wants some of you to do just these things too; but the very first place you are to serve him is in your own home. Let the blessed light of your life be shed abroad in that most sacred of all spots. Brightening that little place, you will be the more ready to be a blessing outside. Those who are the best Christians at home are the best everywhere else.

February 3

KEEPING OUR PROMISES

Many people promise anything you ask of them, but make a small matter of keeping their promises. They enter into engagements with you to do this or that, to meet you or call on you at a certain time or to do some favour for you, and utterly fail to fulfil their engagements. This is a very serious matter this lack of fidelity to promises and engagements. Surely we ought to keep sedulous watch over ourselves in this regard. We ought to be faithful to the promises we make, cost what it may. It is a noble thing when we find one whose promises we are as sure of as of the rising of the sun; whose simplest word is as good as his oath; who does just what he says he will do at the moment he says he will do it. That is the kind of faithfulness God wants.

February 4

LOVE AS WELL AS SERVICE

We may carry too far our idea that all our service of Christ, our acts of love for him, must be also in some way acts of practical beneficence and help to our fellow-men. We may not call all deeds and gifts wasted which do not feed the hungry or clothe the naked. In secret we may pour our broken heart's love upon Christ, bathing his feet with penitential tears, even though we do nothing in these acts for any human life. In our worship we may adore him and love him, though we comfort no sad heart and help no weary one. Nothing is so grateful to the heart of Christ as love, and surely we ought sometimes just to love Christ, forgetting every other being in the ecstasy of our heart's adoring.

February 5

GOD'S PLAN FOR OUR LIVES

God does not merely make souls and send them into this world to take bodies and grow up amid crowds of other souls with bodies, to take their chances and make what they can of their destinies. He plans specifically for each life. He deals with us as individuals. He knows us by name, and loves us each one with a love as distinct and personal as if each was the only child he had on this earth. He has a definite plan for each life. It is always a beautiful plan too, for he never designs marring and ruin for a life. He never made a human soul for the express purpose of being lost. God's design for each life is that it shall reach a holy character, do a good work in the world, fill a worthy place, however humble and fill it well, so as to honour God and bless the world.

February 6

THE HABIT OF SYMPATHY

The gentle ministries of love which you take time to perform as you hurry from task to task in your busy days will give you the sweetest joy as you remember them in the after-days. What these ministries are to those who receive them you never can know till your own heart is sad and lonely and one comes to you in turn with the true comfort of love. Train yourself to the habit of sympathy. Be ready any hour to speak the full rich word of love which shall lighten the burden of the one you meet. Everywhere are hearts that need and hunger for what you have to give, and God has given love to you for the very purpose of blessing those whom he sends to you day by day.

February 7

USE YOUR ONE TALENT

Use your one talent for God's glory, and he will give you more to use. Do the little duties faithfully, and you will grow in skill and ability and be able for greater. No duties are small or unimportant. There are many who grow discouraged because they are kept all their life at little tasks. Men praise grand and heroic deeds, and little notice is taken of the common heroisms of daily duty. But you remember what one said – that if God sent two angels to earth, one to rule an empire and the other to clean a street, they would each regard their employment as equally distinguished. True faithfulness regards nothing as small or unimportant.

February 8

THE COST OF BEING GOOD

We can never bless the world by merely having a good time in it. We must suffer, give, and sacrifice, if we would do good to others. It costs even to be good. Some of us know what self-repression, what self-restraint, what self-crucifixion, and what long, severe discipline lie behind calmness, peacefulness, sweetness of disposition, good-temper, kindly feelings, and habitual thoughtfulness. Most of us have lived long enough to know that these qualities do not come naturally. We have to learn to be good-tempered, thoughtful, gentle, even to be courteous, and the learning is always hard. Indeed we attain nothing good or beautiful in spiritual life without cost.

February 9

'AS I HAVE LOVED YOU'

'Love one another as I have loved you.' How did Christ love his disciples? How did he manifest his love to them? Was it not, among other ways, in wondrous patience with them, with their faults, their ignorance, their unfaithfulness? Was it not in considerate kindness, in ever-watchful thoughtfulness, in compassionate gentleness? Was it not in ministering to them in all possible ways? What is it, then, to love one another as he loves us? Is it not to take his example for our pattern? But how slowly we learn it! How hard it is to be gentle, patient, kindly, thoughtful, even perfectly true and just, one to another! Still, there the lesson stands and waits for us, and we must never falter in learning it.

February 10

SOUL-HUNGER

A religion that is satisfied with any ordinary attainments – indeed, that is ever satisfied at all – is not a living religion. The Master's benediction is upon those that hunger and thirst after righteousness. It is the longing soul that grows. There are better things before you than you have yet attained. Strive to reach them. It is not easy to rise Christward, heavenward, to advance in the Christian life, to grow better. It is hard, costly, painful. Many people are discouraged because they do not appear to themselves to be any better, to be any more like Christ, today than they were yesterday. But even true longing is growth. It is the soul's reaching Godward.

'The thing we long for, that we are
For one transcendent moment.'

February 11

GOD AND NATURE

We talk about laws of nature, and we say they are fixed and unchanging. Yes; but God is behind the laws of nature. They are merely his ways of working. They do not work and grind like a great heartless machine; there is a heart of love, a Father's heart, at the centre of all this vast mechanism which we call nature. All things work together for good to every one who loves God. *You* are the centre of the universe in a sense that is wondrously true. All things revolve about you; all things minister to your good. If only you keep your trust fixed upon God, and are obedient and submissive, even nature's tremendous energies will never harm your true life.

February 12

THE SPLENDOUR OF COMMON DUTY

Every common walk of life is glorious with God's presence, if we could but see the glory. We are always under commission from Christ. We have sealed orders from him every morning, which are opened as the day's events come. Every opportunity for duty or for heroism is a divine call. Be loyal to duty, no matter where you may hear its call nor to what service it may bid you. Duty is duty, however humble it may be; and duty is always nobler, because it is what God himself allots. The work which the day brings to us is always his will, and the sweetest thing in all this world to a loving, loyal heart always is God's will. The service of angels in heaven's brightness is no more radiant than the faithful duty-doing of the lowliest saint on earth.

February 13

THE LOSING THAT IS SAVING

The way to make nothing of our life is to be very careful of it, to hold it back from perilous duty, from costly service, to save it from the waste of self-denial and sacrifice. The way to make our life an eternal success is to do with it what Jesus did with his – present it a living sacrifice to God to be used wholly for him. Men said he threw his life away, and so it certainly seemed up to the morning of his resurrection. But no one would say that now of Christ. His was the throwing away of life which led to its glorifying. In no other way can we make anything worthy and eternal of our life. Saving is losing. It is losing it in devotion to Christ and his service that saves a life for heavenly honour and glory.

February 14

THE VALUE OF THE RESERVE

There is a wide difference between worrying about a possible future of trial and being ready for it if it should come. The former we should never be; the latter we should always seek to be. It is he who is always prepared for emergencies, for the hard pinches, the steep climbing, the sore struggle, that gets through life victoriously. In moral and spiritual things it is the same. It is the reverse that saves us in all final tests – the strength that lies behind what we need in ordinary experiences. Those who daily commune with God, breathing his life into their souls, become strong with that secret, hidden strength which preserves them from falling in the day of trial. They have a 'vessel' from which to refill the lamp when its little cup of oil is exhausted.

February 15

FINDING YOUR MISSION

To find your mission you have to be faithful wherever God puts you for the present. The humbler things he gives in the earlier years are for your training, that you may be ready at length for the larger and particular service for which you were born. Do these smaller, humbler things well, and they will prove steps in the stairs up to the loftier height where your 'mission' waits. To spurn these plainer duties and tasks, and to neglect them, is to miss your mission itself in the end, for there is no way to get to it but by these ladder-rounds of commonplace things which you disdain. You must build your own ladder day by day in the common fidelities.

February 16

SORROW'S COMPENSATIONS

Beyond the river of sorrow there is a promised land. No grief for the present seems joyous, yet afterward it leads to blessing. There is a rich possible good beyond every pain and trial. There are green fields beyond sorrow's Jordans. God never means harm to our lives when he sends afflictions to us. Our disappointments are God's appointments, and bring rich compensation. Our losses are designed to become gains to us as God plans for us. There is nothing really evil in the experiences of a Christian, if only God be allowed to work out the issue. Our Father sends us nothing but good. No matter about the drapery, be is sombre or gay, it unfolds a gift of love.

February 17

A TIME TO BE DEAF

In slander the listener is almost, if not quite, as bad as the speaker. The only true thing is to shut your ears the moment you begin to hear from any one an evil report of another. The person has no right to tell it to you, and you have no right to hear it. If you refuse to listen, he will not be able to go on with his narration. Ears are made to hear with, but on occasion it is well to be deaf. We all aim at courtesy, and courtesy requires that we be patient listeners, even to dull and prosy talkers; but even courtesy may not require us to listen to evil reports about a neighbour. Ear-gate should be trained to shut instinctively when the breath of aspersion touches it, just as eye-gate shuts at slightest approach of harm.

February 18

PERSONAL INFLUENCE

Every human life is a force in this world. On every side our influence pours perpetually. If our lives are true and good, this influence is a blessing to other lives. Let us never set agoing any influence which we shall ever want to have gathered up and buried with us. When we think of our personal influence, unconscious, perpetual, pervading and immortal, can we but cry out, 'Who is sufficient for these things?' How can we command this outflow from our lives that it shall always be blessed? Let us be faithful in all duties, in all obligations and responsibilities, in all obediences, in act, word and disposition, all the days, in whatever makes influence. In no other way can we meet the responsibility of living.

February 19

THE HUMAN PART

The work of seeking, winning, and gathering perishing souls Christ has committed to his disciples. The redemption is divine, but the mediation of it is human. So far as we know, no lost sinner is brought to repentance and faith save through one who already believes. It is the Holy Spirit who draws souls to Christ, yet the Spirit works through believers on unbelievers. We see thus a hint of our responsibility for the saving of the lost souls that our soul touches. There are those who will never be saved unless we do our part to save them. Our responsibility is commensurate with our opportunity. Christ wants daily to pour his grace through us to other lives, and we are ready for this most sacred of all ministries only when we are content to be nothing that Christ may be all in all; vessels emptied that he may fill them; channels through which his grace may flow.

February 20

THE TRUE MINISTRY OF PAIN

There is a Christian art of enduring pain which we should seek to learn. The real problem is not just to endure the suffering which falls into our life, to bear it bravely, without wincing, to pass through it patiently, even rejoicingly. Pain has a higher mission to us than to teach us heroism. We should endure it in such a way as to get something of blessing out of it. It brings to us some message from God which we should not fail to hear. It lifts for us the veil that hides God's face, and we should get some new glimpses of his beauty every time we are called to suffer. Pain is furnace-fire, and we should come out of it always with the gold of our character gleaming a little more brightly. Every experience of suffering ought in some way to lift us nearer God, to make us more gentle and loving, and to leave the image of Christ shining a little clearer in our lives.

February 21

FAULT-FINDING

It is strange how oblivious we can be of our own faults and of the blemishes in our own character, and how clearly we can see the faults and blemishes of other people. Finding so much wrong in others is not a flattering indication of what our hearts contain. We ought to be very quiet and modest in criticising others, for in most cases we are just telling the world what our own faults are. Before we turn our microscopes on others to search out the unbeautiful things in them, we had better look in our mirrors to see whether or not we are free ourselves from the blemishes we would reprove in our neighbour. There is a wise bit of Scripture which bids us get clear of the beams in our own eyes, that we may see well to pick the motes out of the eyes of others.

February 22

MAKING SWEET MEMORIES

We are all making memories in our todays for our tomorrows. The back-log in the old fashioned fireplace sings as it burns, and one with poetic fancy says that the music is the bird-songs of past years – that when the tree was growing in the forest the birds sang in its branches, and the music sank into the tree and was held there, until now in the winter fire it is set free. This is only a beautiful fancy, but there is an analogy in life which is actual. Along the days of childhood and youth the bird-notes of gladness sing about us. They sink away into the heart and hide there. In the busy days of toil and care which follow they oft times seem to be lost and forgotten. Then, in still later days, the fires of trial come and kindle about the life, and in the flames the long-imprisoned music is set free and flows out. Many an old age is brightened and sweetened by the memories of early years. They are wise who in their happy youth-time fill their hearts with pure, pleasant things; they are laying up blessings for old age.

February 23

IN ALL THY WAYS

Do we make much of God in our lives? Is God really much to us in conscious personal experience? Do we not go on making plans and carrying them out without once consulting him? We talk to him about our souls and about our spiritual affairs; but we do not speak to him about our daily work, or trials, our perplexities, our week-day, work-day life. We are to shut God out of no part of our life. We must have something besides human nature, even at its best, if we would be ready for all that lies before us. We must get our little lives so attached to God's life that we can draw from his fulness in every time of need.

February 24

THE BLESSING OF TEMPTATION

We sometimes wish there were no temptation, no sore trial in life, nothing to make it hard to be good, to be true, to be noble, to be pure. But did you ever think that these great qualities can never be gotten easily, without struggle, without self-denial, without toil? Every promised land in life lies beyond a deep, turbulent river, which must be crossed before the beautiful land can be entered. Not to be able to cross the stream is not to enter the blessed country. Every temptation is therefore a path which leads to something noble and good. If we endure the temptation and are victorious, we shall find ourselves within the gates of a new paradise. 'Blessed is the man that endureth temptation: for when he hath been approved, he shall receive the crown of life, which the Lord promised to them that love him.'

February 25

FIDELITY IN TRIFLES

There will be honours eternal for those who have filled important places of trust and responsibility in this world and have proved faithful in great things. There will be crowns of glory for the martyrs who, along the ages, have died rather than deny Christ. But there will be rewards just as brilliant and diadems just as splendid for those who, in lives of lowly service and self-denial and in patient endurance and humble devotion, have been faithful in the things that are least. God does not overlook the lowly, nor does he forget the little things. If only we are faithful in the place to which he assigns us and in the duties he gives us, we shall have our reward, whether the world praises, or whether our lives and our deeds are unknown and unpraised among men. Faithful! that is the approval which brings glory.

February 26

POWER AND RESPONSIBILITY

Power makes responsibility. You are not responsible merely for what you are trying to do, but for what God has given you power to do. Wake up those slumbering possibilities in your soul; you are responsible for all these. Stir up the unused, inactive gifts that are in you; you are responsible for these. The things you can do, or can learn to do, are the things Christ is calling you to do, and the things he will require at your hand when he comes again. It is time we were understanding life's meaning. God gives us seeds, but he will require more than seeds at our hand; he will require all the harvest of beauty and blessing that the best tillage can bring out of the seeds.

February 27

THE MINISTRY OF SYMPATHY

No ministry in this world is more beautiful or more helpful than that of those who have become familiar with life's paths, and have learned life's secrets in the school of experience, and then go about inspiring, strengthening, and guiding younger souls who come after them. Nothing in Christ is more precious than this knowledge of life's ways, gained by his own actual experience in human paths. He has not forgotten what life was to him. He remembers how he felt when he was hungry, or weary, or in struggle with the tempter, or forsaken by his friends. And it is because he passed through all these experiences that now in heaven he can be touched with the feeling of our infirmities, and can give us sympathy, help and guidance.

February 28

GROWING THROUGH HABITS

One whose daily life is careless is always weak; but one who habitually walks in the paths of uprightness and obedience grows strong in character. Exercise develops all the powers of his being. Doing good continually adds to one's capacity for doing good. Victoriousness in trial or trouble puts ever new strength into the heart. The habit of faith in the darkness prepares for stronger faith. Habits of obedience make one immovable in one's loyalty to duty. We can never over-estimate the importance of life's habits; they lead our growth of character in whatever way they tend.

February 29

'THY WILL BE DONE'

God's will for us leads on earth to the noblest, truest, most Christ-like character, and then beyond this world to glory and eternal life. For you, whatever your experiences, however hard and painful life may seem to you, God's will is the very hand of divine love to lead you on toward all that is good and beautiful and blessed. Never doubt it, even in the darkest hour, or when the pain is sorest, or when the cross is heaviest. God's will holds you ever close to God, and leads you ever toward and into God's sweetest rest. It brings peace to the heart – a peace that never can come in any way of our own choosing – to be able always to say, 'Thy will be done.'

MARCH

March 1

LOVE'S MINISTRY

Love's quality is measured by what it will do, what it will give, what it will suffer. God so loved the world that he gave – gave his only-begotten Son, gave all, withheld nothing. That is the measure of the divine love for us: it loves to the uttermost. If you are Christ's, every energy of your mind, every affection of your heart, every power of your soul, every fibre of your body, every particle of your influence, every penny of your money, is Christ's, and all of these are to be used to bless your fellow-men and to make the world better and happier. If we love, we will give, we will suffer, we will sacrifice. If we would be like God, we must live to minister, giving our life, without reserve, to service in Christ's name.

March 2

BEFORE THE SUN GOES DOWN

Estrangements between friends should not be permitted to continue over night. It is a scriptural counsel that we should not let the sun go down upon our wrath. Why? Because there may not be another day in which to get the would healed and the estrangement removed. 'But it was not my fault,' you say. Noble souls, inspired by the love of Christ, must not ask whose fault it was that the estrangement began, nor whose place it is first to seek restoration. If it was not your fault, your are the better one to begin the reconciliation. It is Christ-like for the one who is not to blame to take the first step toward the healing of the breach, That is the way He did and always does with us. Do not delay too long. What time is it? Is the sun moving toward his setting? Hasten, and before the shadows of evening come on be reconciled with your friend. Let not the stars look down on two hearts sundered by anger or misunderstanding.

March 3

GREATNESS IN GOD'S SIGHT

The greatest men are but fractions of men. No one is endowed with all gifts. Every one has his own particular excellence or ability. No two have precisely the same gifts, and no two are called to fill precisely the same place in life. The lowliest and the humblest in endowments is just as important in his place as the most brilliantly gifted. The great life in God's sight is not the conspicuous one, but the life that fills the place which it was made to do. God asks not great things; he asks only simple faithfulness, the quiet doing of what he allots.

March 4

MINOR UNTRUTHFULNESS

There are other forms of untruthfulness besides the direct lie. There are those who would not speak an untrue word, who yet colour their statements so as to make them really false in the impression they leave; or they would not speak a lie, but they will act one. Their lives are full of small deceits, concealments, pretences, insincerities, dissimulations, dishonesties. You know how many of these there are in society. Oh, be true in your inmost soul – true in every word, act, look, tone and feeling. Never deceive. There are no white lies in God's sight; it is a miserable fiction that thinks there are.

March 5

TODAY, NOT TOMORROW

There are duties that must be done at a particular moment or they cannot be done at all! It is today the sick neighbour needs your visit, your help; tomorrow he may be well or others will have ministered to him, or he may be dead. It is today that your friend needs your sympathy, your comfort; it will not be of any use to him tomorrow. It is today that this tempted one needs your help in his struggle; tomorrow he may be defeated, lying in the dust of shame. It is today you must tell the story of the love of Christ; tomorrow it may be too late. Learn well the meaning of Now in all life. Tomorrow is a fatal word; thousands of lives and countless thousands of hopes have been wrecked on it. Today is the word of divine blessing.

March 6

TRUSTING FOR TOMORROW

Should the uncertainty of all human affairs sadden our lives? No; God does not want us to bring tomorrow's possible clouds to shadow our todays. He does not want us to be unhappy while the sun shines because by-and-by it will be dark. He wants us to live in today and enjoy its blessings and do its work well, though tomorrow may bring calamity. How can we? Only by calm, quiet, trustful faith in God and obedience to him at every step. Then no troublous tomorrow can ever bring us harm. Those who do God's will each day God will hide under his wings when the storm breaks.

March 7

THE BEAUTY WITHIN

Bodily health is beautiful. Mental vigour is beautiful. But heart-purity is the glory of all loveliness. The heart makes the life. The inner fashions the outer. So, above all things, be pure-hearted. That you may be pure-hearted let Christ more and more into your life, that he may fill all your soul, and that his Spirit may permeate all your being. That the beauty of the Lord may be upon you, that the winning charm of God's loveliness may shine in your features, you must first have the beauty of Christ within you. The transfiguration must come from within. Only a holy, beautiful heart can make a holy, beautiful character.

March 8

ANSWERS THAT WAIT

The day may come to us, as life's meaning deepens, when we shall cry to Christ and he will not seem to hear. Whenever this experience may come, let us remember that Christ's silence is not refusal to bless. There may be some hindrance in ourselves, and a work of preparation is needed in us before the blessing can come. Instead of doubting or blaming the Master, we should look within ourselves and ask what it is that keeps the answer waiting. When we are down lower in the dust of humiliation, when our weak faith has grown stronger, when our self-will is gone and we are ready to take the blessing in God's way and at his time, the silence will be broken by love's most gracious answer.

March 9

CHARACTER-BUILDING

That picture of the silent temple-builders on Mount Moriah is the picture of all the good work of the world. Ever the builders are at work on these characters of ours, but they work silently. From a thousand sources come the little blocks that are laid upon the walls. The lessons we get from others, the influences which friends exert upon us, the truths which reading puts into our minds, the impressions which life leaves upon us, the inspirations from the divine Spirit – in all these ways the silent work of building goes on. It never ceases. The builders never rest. By day and by night the character-temple is rising. Is it all beautiful? Are the stones all clean and white?

March 10

STRONGEST WITH THE WEAKEST

We are not all alike temptable. There are some with sweet temper and equable disposition whom nothing disturbs. God seems to have sheltered them by their very nature from the power of evil. Then there are others whose natures seem to be open on all sides, exposed to every danger. To live truly costs them fierce struggles every day. These easily-tempted ones are they to whom Christ's sympathy and helpfulness go out in most tender interest. He singles out the one from every circle that is most liable to fall, and makes special intercession for that one. Even the Johns with their gentle loveliness, receive less of help from the Master than do the fiery Peters.

March 11

WEAKNESS OF LITTLE FAITH

It is because of our lack of faith, or of our small faith, that there is so little outcome from our ceaseless rounds of doing. If we had the power of Christ resting upon us as we might have it, with one-tenth of the activity, there would be ten times the result. Only think of the possibilities of our lives, the plainest, commonest of them, if we had all of Christ that we might have! He is ready to do through us greater things than he himself did. We need faith to lay ourselves in Christ's hand as the chisel lays itself in the hand of the sculptor. Then every touch of ours will produce beauty in some life. Then all the power of Christ will work through us.

March 12

THE SANCTITY OF CONSECRATED LIFE

The soul that has had a vision of the Christ, the person in whom Christ is already formed the 'hope of glory', and who is also himself destined to wear the divine image, must never drag his honour in the dust of sin, must never degrade his holy powers in any evil service. Every time we are tempted to commit some sin, if we would stop and think, 'I am now a child of God; shall a child of God, destined to wear Christ's image, stoop to be untrue or dishonest or impure, or to cherish wrath or bitterness?' would we not turn away from the temptation? Could we sin against God with the consciousness of our high calling in our heart?

March 13

THE LAW OF AMUSEMENTS

Amusements are proper, both as to kind and degree, just so far as they make us better Christians. Whenever they become hindrances to us in our Christian living or in our progress in sanctification, they are harmful, however innocent they may be in themselves. How do your amusements act on your spiritual life? What is their influence on you? They may be very pleasing to you. They may afford great gratification. But what is their effect on you as a Christian? In one word, Are they means of grace? Or are they making you careless for Christ and hindering your advancement in spirituality? We ought to be honest enough with ourselves to answer these questions truthfully, and then act accordingly.

March 14

THE ELOQUENCE OF LIVING

Tongues of angels without love to inspire their silvery strains are but as tinkling cymbals. Life itself is infinitely more potent than speech. Character far surpasses elocution as a force in this world. The talking standard is a false one in the estimating of the value and power of Christian workers. Do what you have gifts to do. Be sure of your heart-life. Make your personal character a sublime force in the world. Then when the accents of silvery speech shall have died away, your influence will still remain a living power in the hearts of men and an unfading light in the world.

March 15

WHAT TO DO WITH INJURIES

What must we do with the wrongs and injustices and injuries inflicted upon us by others if we are not to avenge them? How are these wrongs to be righted and these injuries to be healed? Do not fear the consequences of any wrong done to you. Simply roll the matter into God's hands and leave it there, and he will bring all out clear as the noonday. He will not suffer us to be permanently and really injured by any enmity. Our duty, then, is to bear meekly and patiently the suffering which others may cause us to endure; to bathe with love the hand that smites; to forgive those who injure us; and to commit all the injustices and inequities of our lives and all wrongs into the hand of the just and righteous God. The oyster's wounds become pearls; and God can bring pearls of spiritual beauty out of the hurts made by human hands in our lives.

March 16

LEARNING MEEKNESS

Religion is not good believing only; it is getting the good things of good men and of God down out of the old pages of inspiration where we find them and into our own lives. Meekness as a beatitude is very beautiful. Meekness in Moses we admire greatly. But how much of it are we getting out of beatitude and biography into the experience of these common days? In our daily intercourse with men do we hold our hearts quiet and still under all harshness, rudeness, criticism, injustice? There are countless little irritations and provocations that make friction every day. How do we endure them? Do they polish and refine our natures? These are the lessons of meekness.

March 17

SILENCE THAT IS GOLDEN

It is easy for one to poison a person's mind concerning another. There is measureless ruin wrought in this world by the slanderer. Characters are blackened, friendships are destroyed, jealousies are aroused, homes are torn up, hearts are broken. Let us never take up an evil report and give it wing on breath of ours. Let us never whisper an evil thing of another. We know not where it may end, to what it may grow, what ruin it may work. Words once spoken can never be gotten back again. We had better learn to keep the door of our lips locked and say no evil ever of any one. This is a silence we shall never regret.

March 18

THE SHADOW OF GOD'S WINGS

Is there a grief in your heart which groweth into a sore pain? Is there a shadow of a coming sorrow that you see drooping down over you? Remember it is the shadow of God's wing, and therefore it is a safe shadow. Creep closer under it, closer yet. Earth has nothing human so gentle as true mother-love; but God's wing that folds down over you then is gentler than even mother-love; and you can never get out from beneath it. It holds you close to the gentle heart of the divine Father. You need never be afraid while resting there. In all the universe there is no harm that can come nigh you. From your eternal shelter you can look out with confidence, as from a window of heaven, on the fury of earth's storms, and be at peace. The wildest of them cannot touch you in your pavilion.

March 19

THE BEAUTY OF RELIGION

While Christian life is firm and unflinching in its integrity and uprightness, it is yet beautiful in its amiability and gentleness. The immutable principles of uprightness, like mountain-crags, are wreathed over with the tender vines and covered with the sweet flowers of grace and charity. True religion is never meant to dry up the life and make it cold, hard and dead. It is meant to bring out ever-new beauties, to clothe the soul in garments of loveliness. It insists on the development of every power of body, mind and soul to the farthest possibility. It presents the strongest motives. It points to the finest examples. Its ideal includes not only 'whatsoever things are true, whatsoever things are just,' but also 'whatsoever things are lovely.'

March 20

SELF-RENUNCIATION

They are highest in the ranks of men who serve, who live for others, whose lives are given out in loving, unselfish ministry; and they rank highest of all who serve the most deeply and unselfishly. It is only in serving that we begin to be like the angels and like God himself. It is when the worker for Christ utterly forgets himself, sacrifices himself in the fire of his love for Christ, that his labour for souls yields the richest and best results. When we care only that Christ may be magnified, whether by honour or dishonour, by life or death, in us, then will he honour us by using us to win souls for his kingdom.

March 21

SAYING 'YES' TO CHRIST

To believe on Christ as a disciple is to say 'Yes' to him always, with the whole heart, with the whole being. It is giving up the sins that grieve him. It is cutting loose from whatever displeases him. It is renouncing every other master, and taking orders from him only. It is going with him, following him wherever he leads, without question, without condition, without reserve, not counting the cost. It is saying 'Yes' to Christ whatever he may ask us to do or to give up or to sacrifice or to suffer. That was the way his first disciples followed him. That is the way his disciples must follow him now. Absolute obedience to him is the condition of following.

March 22

'UNTO THE END'

The most wonderful thing in the universe is our Saviour's love for his own. Christ bears with all our infirmities. He never tires of our inconsistencies and unfaithfulnesses. He goes on for ever forgiving and forgetting. He follows us when we go astray. He does not forget us when we forget him. Through all our stumbling and sinning, through all our provocation and disobedience, through all our waywardnesses and stubbornnesses, through all our doubting and unfaithfulness, he clings to us still, and never lets us go. Having loved his own, he loves unto the end.

March 23

'AFTERWARD'

In the divine providence nothing comes a moment too soon or to late, but everything comes in its own true time. God's clock is never too slow. Every link of the chain of God's providences fits into its own place. We do not see the providence at the time. Not until afterward you will see that your disappointments, hardships, trials, and the wrongs inflicted on you by others, are parts of God's good providence toward you, full of blessing. Not until afterward will you see it, but the 'afterward' is sure if you firmly and faithfully follow Christ and cleave to him. The 'afterward' of every disappointment or sorrow is blessing and good. We need only to learn to wait in patience.

March 24

VICTORY BY YIELDING

Jacob got the victory and the blessing not by wrestling, but by clinging. His limb was out of joint and he could struggle no longer, but he would not let go. Unable to wrestle, he wound his arms around the neck of his mysterious antagonist and hung all his helpless weight upon him, until at last he conquered. We will not get victory in prayer until we too cease our struggling, give up our own will and throw our arms about our Father's neck in clinging faith. What can puny human strength take by force out of the hand of Omnipotence? Can we wrest blessings by force from God? It is never the violence of wilfulness that prevails with God. It is the might of clinging faith that gets the blessings and the victories. It is not when we press and urge our own will, but when humility and trust unite in saying, 'Not my will, but thine.' We are strong with God only in the degree that self is conquered and is dead. Not by wrestling, but by clinging, can we get the blessing.

March 25

THE LESSON OF PEACE

Where Christ places us we are to remain; where he sends us we are to go; and in the heat of life's conflicts, set upon on every hand by a host of things which tend to distract our peace, we are to maintain an unruffled calm and all the tenderness and simplicity of the heart of a little child. That is the problem of life and of living which Christ sets for us, and which he will help us to solve if we accept him as our teacher. As the tender grass and even sweet flowers live and grow all through the winter under the deep snows, and come forth in the spring-time in beauty, so our hearts may remain loving, tender, and joyous through life's sorest winter under the snows of trial and sorrow.

March 26

CLIMBING UPWARD

Some one asked an old minister, 'What is repentance?' 'The first turn to the right,' was his answer. If you want to grow into Christlikeness, rising at length into radiant purity and sainthood, you must begin with the first simple duty that comes to your hand. Resist the first temptation. Do the first right thing that offers. Paint on your soul the first vision of divine loveliness you see. You cannot reach sainthood at the bound; you must conquer your way up step by step:

'Heaven is not reached by a single bound,
But we build the ladder by which we rise,
From the lowly earth to the vaulted skies,
And we mount to its summit round by round.'

March 27

ALWAYS OUR BEST

All Christ wants from any of us is what we have ability to do. He asks no impossibilities. He accepts our homeliest, poorest gifts or services if they are indeed our best and if true love to him consecrates and sanctifies them. We need to care but for two things – that we do always our best, and that we do what we do through love for Christ. If we are faithful up to the measure of our ability and opportunity, and if love sanctifies what we do, we are sure of our Lord's approval. But we should never offer less than the best that we can do; to do so is to be disloyal to our Lord and disloyal to our own soul.

March 28

'THINKETH NO EVIL'

Love thinketh no evil. It does not suspect unkindness in kindly deeds. It does not imagine an enemy in every friend. It does not fear insincerity in sincere professions of esteem. It does not impugn men's motives nor discount their acts. On the other hand, it overlooks foibles and hides the multitude of faults that belong to every human being, even those who are the holiest and the best. It believes in the good that is in people, and tries to think of them always at their best, not at their worst. It looks, too, at the possibilities that are in men, what they may become through divine love and grace, and not merely at what they now are. It is wonderful how seeing through love's eyes changes the whole face of earthly life, transfiguring it. If the heart be filled with suspicion, distrust, and doubt of men, the world grows very ugly. But love sees brightness, beauty, and hope everywhere.

March 29

NEED A REVEALER OF LOVE

Whatever makes us forget ourselves and think of others lifts us upward. This is one reason that God permits suffering. We would never know the best and richest of human love if there were no pain, no distress, no appeal of grief or of need. The best and holiest of mother-love would never be brought out if the child never suffered. The same is true of God's love. God would have loved his children unfallen just as much as he loves them fallen, but the world would never have known so much of God's love had not man fallen. Our sore need called out all that was richest, holiest, and divinest in our Father's heart. If no night came we should never know there are stars. Darkness is a revealer.

March 30

FAITHFULNESS

Whatever your duty is, you cannot be faithful to God unless you do your work as well as you can. To slur it is to do God's work badly. To neglect it is to rob God. The universe is not quite complete without your little work well done. 'Be thou faithful' is the word that rings from heaven in every ear, in every smallest piece of work we are doing. 'Faithful' as a measure of requirement is not a pillow for indolence. It is not a letting down of obligation to a low standard to make life easy. Faithfulness is a lofty standard. It means our very best and most always. Anything less is unfaithfulness. Thus the universe suffers, for the smallest duty not done or badly done leaves a lack or a blemish on the whole world's work.

March 31

BLESSED TO BE A BLESSING

God blesses you that you may be a blessing to others. Then he blesses you also a second time in being a blessing to others. It is the talent that is used that multiplies. Receiving, unless one gives in turn, makes one full and proud and selfish. Give out the best of your life in the Master's name for the good of others. Lend a hand to every one who needs. Be ready to serve at any cost those who require your service. Seek to be a blessing to every one who comes for but a moment under your influence. This is to be angel-like. It is to be Godlike. It is to be Christlike. We are in this world to be useful. God wants to pass his gifts and blessing through us to others. When we fail as his messengers, we fail of our mission.

APRIL

April 1

GOD HIMSELF HIS OWN BEST GIFT

Enlarge your desires and your prayers. Do not ask merely for mercies and favours and common gifts. Do not ask God merely to give you bread, and health, and home, and friends, and prosperity; or, rising yet a step higher, do not content yourself with asking for grace to help in temptation, or for strength to fill up your weakness, or for wisdom to guide you in perplexity, or for holiness and purity and power. Ask for God himself, and then open your heart to receive him. If you have God, you have all other gifts and blessings in him. And it is himself that God is willing to give for the asking, not merely the favours and benefits that his hand dispense. Ask most largely.

April 2

A BEAUTIFUL LIFE

A life need not be great to be beautiful. There may be as much beauty in a tiny flower as in a majestic tree, in a little gem as in a great mountain, in the smallest creature as in a mammoth. A life may be very lovely and yet be insignificant in the world's eyes. A beautiful life is one that fulfils its mission in this world, that is what God made it to be, and does what God made it to do. Those with only commonplace gifts are in danger of thinking that they cannot live a beautiful life, cannot be a blessing in this world. But the smallest life that fills its place well is far lovelier in God's sight than the largest and most splendidly gifted that yet fails of its divine mission.

> 'Far better in its place the lowliest bird
>   Should sing aright to Him the lowliest song,
> Than that a seraph strayed should take the word
>   And sing his glory wrong.'

April 3

FOLLOWING OUR WHITE BANNERS

We talk about consecration. What is consecration? It is nothing less than doing the will of Christ, not our own, always, whatever the cost, the sacrifice, or the danger. There is too much mere sentiment in our religion. We say we believe in Christ; if we do, we must follow him wherever he leads, though not knowing whither. We say we love Christ, and quickly from his lips comes the testing word – 'If ye love me, keep my commandments.' To be a Christian is to be devoted utterly, resistlessly, irrevocably, to Christ. Joan of Arc said the secret of her victoriousness was that she bade her white standard go forth boldly; then she followed it herself. Good intentions, and vows, and pledges of consecration are well enough as white banners, but when we have sent them forth we must be sure to follow them ourselves.

April 4

'AS THY DAYS'

There is in the Bible no promise of grace in advance of the need. God does not say he will put strength into our arm for the battle while we are in quiet peace and the battle is yet far off. When the conflict is at hand the strength will be given. He does not open the gates for us, nor roll away the stones, until we have come up to them. He did not divide the Jordan's waters while the people were yet in their camps, nor even as they began to march toward the river. The wild stream continued to flow as the host moved down the banks, even until the feet of the priests had been dipped in the water. This is the constant law of divine help. It is not given in advance. As we come up to the need the supply is ready, but not before. Yet many Christians worry because they cannot see the way opened and the needs supplied far in advance of their steps. Shall we not let God provide and have faith in him?

Keep thou my feet; I do not ask to see
The distant scene; one step enough for me.'

April 5

TRUE WOMANHOOD

That is not Christ's religion which is moved to ecstasies of love and compassion for the Zulus and Chinese across seas, and is selfish, irritable, greedy, impatient and disobliging at home. The true woman is the very soul of self-forgetfulness in her own home-circle. Then wherever she goes she is the same. She carries the sweet, patient spirit of Christ everywhere. Her hands are gentle as an angel's, and are ever scattering blessings. Her words are thrilled with a strange power of sympathy and tenderness, and carry comfort into the sad heart, courage into the fainting heart, life into the sluggish heart. A selfish woman is a contradiction. Wherever selfishness does appear in a woman it is a blur that disfigures the divine beauty.

April 6

TURNING VISIONS INTO LIFE

God gives us visions of spiritual beauty that we may turn them into realities in common life. All our heavenward aspirations we should bring down and work into acts. All our longings and desires we should make true in experiences. Every day's Bible text taken into the heart should shine forth tomorrow in some new touch of spiritual beauty. As the look of the face is caught in the camera and held there, so every time Christ looks in upon our souls, even for an instant, some impression of his features should become fixed there, and remain as part of our spiritual beauty, So in all our life the words of Christ we hear, the lessons we are taught, and the holy influences that touch our souls, should enter into our very being and reappear in disposition, character, deeds.

April 7

OTHER PEOPLE'S FAULTS

No doubt it is easier to discover other people's faults than our own. Many of us are troubled more about the way our neighbours live, than we are with our own shortcomings. We manifest a greater feeling of responsibility for the acts and neglects of others than for our own. Now, the truth is, every man bear his own burden. We shall not be called to answer at God's bar for the idle words, the sinful acts, and the neglects of duty of our neighbour. But there is one person for whose every act, word, disposition, and feeling we shall have to give an account, and that is ourself. We had better train ourselves, therefore, to keep close, minute, incessant, and conscientious watch over our own life. We had better give less attention to our neighbour's mistakes, foibles, and failures, and more to our own. Most of us would find little time for looking after other people's faults if we have strict attention to our own. Besides, seeing and knowing our own defects would make us more charitable to those of others.

April 8

THE FATHERHOOD OF GOD

How it would brighten and bless our lives if we were to carry always in our hearts the conception of God as our Father! When we can look up into God's face and say out of warm and responding hearts, 'Our Father,' all the world and all life take on new aspect for our eyes. Duty is no longer hard and a drudgery, but becomes a joy. Keeping the commandments is hard if we think of God merely as a king; but if we look up to him as our Father, all is changed, and our love for him, and our desire to please him, make obedience a gladness. We can say then, 'I delight to do thy will, O my God.'

April 9

IN THE DISCOURAGED DAYS

We all have our discouraged days, when things do not go well.
The young people fail in their lessons at school, although they
have studied hard and really have done their best. The mothers
are tried in their household work. The children are hard to
control. It has seemed impossible to keep good temper, to
maintain that sweetness and that lovingness which are so
essential to a happy day. Try as they will to be gentle, kindly,
patient, their minds are ruffled. They come to the close of the
long, unhappy hours disturbed, defeated, discouraged. They
have done their best, but they feel that they have really failed.
They fall upon their knees with only tears for a prayer. But if
they will lift up their eyes, they will see on the shore of the
troubled sea of their little day's life the form of One whose
presence will give them strength and confidence, and who will
help them to victoriousness. Before his sweet smile the shadows
flee away; at his word new strength is given, and after that,
work is easy and all goes well again.

April 10

BLESSING IN MISTAKES

Our very mistakes and our sins, if we repent of them, will be
used of God to help in the growth and upbuilding of our
character. Our very falls, through the grace and tender love of
Christ, become new births to our souls.

'Of our vices we can frame
A ladder, if we will but tread
Beneath our feet each deed of shame.'

In the hot fires of penitence we leave the dross and come again
as pure gold. But we must remember that it is only Christ who

can make our sins yield blessing. If we are Christ's true followers, even our defeats shall become blessings to us, stepping-stones on which we may climb higher. This is one of the marvels of divine grace, that it can make all things work together for good.

April 11

SPEAK OUT THE LOVING WORDS

How much better would it be if we were more generous and lavish of our good words when our friends can be cheered and blessed by them! Sometimes we get the lesson of keeping silence over-learned, and let hearts starve for lack of kindly words which lie meanwhile on our tongues ready to be spoken. It is not the want of love for which we are to be blamed, but the penuriousness that locks up the love and will not give it out in word and act to bless hungry lives. Is any other miserliness so mean? We let hearts starve close beside us when we have the bread to feed them, and then, when they lie in the dust of defeat or death, we come with our love to speak eloquent funeral eulogies. Would it not be far better to give out the kindliness when it will do good?

> Why do we wait, and coldly stint our praises,
>   And leave our reverent homage unexpressed,
> Till brave hearts lie beneath a roof of daisies,
>   Then heap with flowers each hallowed place of rest?
>
> For every year the veteran ranks are broken,
>   And every year new graves await our flowers;
> Ah! why not give to living hearts some token
>   Of half the love and pride that throb through ours?
>
> Bring blooms to crown the dead; but, in your giving,
>   Forget not hearts that still can strive and ache:
> O give your richest garlands to the living,
>   Who offered all, in youth, for honour's sake!

April 12

CHRISTIAN WORK

Bring every grace and gift of your life into Christ's service. Not only use well the gifts you have now at work, but develop what you have into greater skill and power of service. Strive ever to excel. Grow by working. Don't stand with idle hands a moment, because for each moment you must give account. Do not allow your spiritual powers to rest in dusty niches merely for adornment. Take them all down and put life into them, that they may be useful. Do not play at Christian work. The King's business requireth haste.

April 13

CHARACTER ALONE ABIDES

We must strive to realize every dream of goodness and Christ-likeness that our hearts dream. Remember it is character that is the only test, and the only true fruit, of living. It is not knowledge; for knowledge will fail. It is not money; for money cannot be carried away from earth. It is not fame; for fame's laurels fade at the grave's edge, and its voice gives no cheer in the valley of shadows. It is not culture or education or refinement. It is life – not what we have or what we know, but what we are – that we can carry with us into the eternal world.

April 14

THE HOME FRIENDSHIPS

Friendships in the family require most gentle care and cultivation. We must win each other's love within home-doors just as we win the love of those outside – by the sweet ministries and graces of affection. We must prove ourselves worthy of being loved by those who are nearest; they will not truly love us unless we do, merely because we are of the same household. We must show ourselves unselfish, thoughtful, gentle, helpful. Home friendships must be formed as all friendships are formed – by the patient knitting of soul to soul and the slow growing of life into life. Then we must retain home-friends after winning just as we retain other friends – by a thousand little winning expressions in all our intercourse. We cannot depend upon relationship to keep us loved and loving. We must live for each other. We must give as well as receive. We must be watchful of our acts and words.

April 15

THE HEART'S DAILY BREAD

We all need sympathy, human kindness, cheer, fellowship, the thousand little things of human love, as we go along the dusty road of life. These small coins of affection are the brighteners of every life that is blessed by a rich friendship. It is this unceasing ministry that your heart hungers for as its daily bread – not great gifts and large favours, but a gentle affectionateness in your friend which shall bring cheer, satisfying, inspiration, comfort, uplifting, hope, and strength to your soul every time you look into his face.

April 16

'IN HIS NAME'

If we have the true spirit of service, we will look upon every one we meet, even casually, as one to whom we owe some debt of love, one sent to us to receive some benediction, some cheer, some comfort, some strength, some inspiration, some touch of beauty at our hand. We may never do one great or conspicuous thing of which men will talk, or which will be reported in the newspapers, but every word we speak, every smallest act, every influence we send out, even unconsciously, 'in His name', merely our shadow falling on human need and pain and sorrow as we pass by, will prove sweet and blessed ministry of love, and will impart strength and help. The name of Christ consecrates every smallest deed or influence, pouring it full of love.

April 17

'I SAY WHAT I THINK'

There is a class of people who boast of their honesty and frankness because they 'just say what they think', flinging out the words right and left as they come, no matter where they strike or whom they wound. Call it not honesty, this boasted frankness; call it rather miserable impertinence, reckless cruelty. We have no right to say what we think unless we think lovingly and sweetly. We certainly have no right to unlade our jealousies, envies, bad humours, and miserable spites upon our neighbour's heart. If we must be ugly-tempered, we should at least keep the ugliness locked up in our own breast, and not let it out to mar other people's happiness. Of, if we must speak out the wretched feelings, let us go into our own room and lock the door and close the windows, that no ears but our own shall hear the hateful words.

April 18

THE PEACEMAKER'S BEATITUDE

It is very easy, if you are talking to one who has a little distrust of another or a little bitterness against another, to say a word which will increase the distrust or add to the bitterness. We like to approve and justify the one with whom we are speaking, and in doing so we are apt to confirm him in his bitterness or sense of wrong. Let us be on our guard that we do not unintentionally widen little rifts into great breaches. Let us seek ever to be peacemakers. There is no other beatitude whose blessing is more radiant than that of the peacemakers – 'they shall be called sons of God.'

April 19

THE BLESSING OF STRUGGLE

The daily temptations which make every true life such a painful conflict from beginning to end bring us constant opportunities for growth of character. Not to struggle is not to grow strong. The soldier's art can be learned and the soldier's honours can be won only on the field of battle. If you would grow into the beauty of the Master, you must accept the conflicts and fight the battles. You can have life easy if you will by declining every struggle, but you will then get little out of life that is truly noble and worthy. The best things all lie beyond some battle-plain: you must fight your way across the field to get them. Heaven is only for those who overcome. None get the crown without the conflict save those who are called home in infancy and early childhood.

'Sure I must fight if I would reign.'

April 20

MINISTRY OF 'SHUT-INS'

A faith that fails not nor murmurs in hours of suffering is like a heavenly lamp burning in the home. It makes the chamber of pain a little sanctuary, a holy of holies, which none can enter but with quiet reverence. Do you think such suffering, so sustained, so radiant, performs no ministry of blessing for those who witness it? We must not think that when God lays us aside from active service, shuts us in and calls us to suffer, he is stopping our usefulness for the time. Besides the enriching of our own lives for new ministries when we come again from the shadows, our suffering may become meanwhile a school for other lives, our faith and peace unspoken sermons on the power of God's love and grace.

April 21

CONSCIENCE IN LITTLE THINGS

Scrupulous people are often laughed at for their scruples. 'Why be so particular?' gay and giddy ones ask. 'Why be so conscientious about mere trifles? Why be so exacting and punctilious in the doing of small duties?' The answer is that in the matter of right and wrong nothing is little; certainly nothing is insignificant. Duty is duty, whether it be the smallest or the greatest matter. He is on the highway to nobleness of character who has learned to be scrupulous concerning the smallest things. He that is careful in little things rises every day a step higher. He who is faithful in little things is then intrusted with larger responsibilities. It is the units in life that are most important. Look after the little units and the greater aggregates will be right. Make the minutes beautiful and the hours and days will be radiant.

April 22

GOODNESS IN THE SHADOWS

Shall we trust our Father only when he is giving us pleasant things, and shall we not trust him also when he brings the shadow over our hearts? Do you think God is good only when he makes all things such as please you? Is he not just as good when he gives you pain or losses? It is the will of God that our home-sorrow shall make our home-life sweeter, purer, kindlier, Christlier. If we believe in God and take the pain from his hand with the same confidence as the pleasure, then the shadows will be as rich blessings to us as the lights and the sorrows will be steps upward on which our feet may climb toward God.

April 23

CHRISTIAN HISTORY

Christian history is one of the best evidences of the deity of Christ. No mere man could touch the world's life as Jesus Christ has touched it. It is nothing less than the energy of God working in men's hearts that has produced the marvellous results which we see wherever the gospel has gone. Men's bodies may not now be instantaneously healed by a divine touch, but men's moral lives are transformed by the same divine touch as in the old miracles of gospel days. Nations are lifted up into purity, justice, truth, freedom and righteousness. Are not these great moral and spiritual miracles as wonderful attestations of the divine mission of Christ as the physical miracles that marked the days of the incarnation?

April 24

COST OF BEING A BLESSING

We must live deeply ourselves if we would be able to bless others. We must resist sin, even unto blood, if we would teach others how to be victorious in temptation. We must bear trials and endure sorrows with patience, with submission, and with faith, so as to be victorious, if we would become comforters and helpers of others in their trials. You must learn before you can teach, and the learning costs. At no small price can we become true helpers of others sin this world. That which has cost us nothing in the getting will not be any great blessing to any other person in the giving. It is only when we lose our life, sacrifice it to God, that we become deeply and truly useful.

April 25

MAKING OTHERS HAPPY

The world needs nothing more than it needs happiness-makers. There is a great deal of sadness everywhere. The Bible is a book meant to make people happy. Joy-bells ring all through it. The mission of the gospel is to make happiness. The angel's announcement of good tidings of great joy is going forth yet on every breeze. The story of the love of Christ is changing darkness to light, despair to hope, tears to laughter, sorrow to rejoicing, in all lands. It is the mission of every Christian to be a happiness-maker. Each one of us has power, too, to add something at least to the world's gladness. We can do this in a thousand ways – by being joyful Christians ourselves, making our lives a sweet song; by telling others the joyful things of the Word of God; by doing kindnesses to all we meet; by comforting sorrow, lifting burdens away, cheering sadness and weariness, and scattering benedictions wherever we go.

April 26

OUR HEART CHRIST'S KINGDOM

Religion is not an art nor a science; it is a life. It is not the mere learning and following of a set of rules. It is the growth of Christ-likeness in the heart, spreading thence into the whole of the being. It is the setting up of the kingdom of heaven within us. This kingdom in one's heart is the rule and authority of Christ, owned and recognized there at the fount and spring of the life. It is the rule of love – 'the love of Christ constraineth me.' St. Paul goes still further, however, and speaks of it as a new incarnation. 'Christ liveth in me,' he says. A Christian life is therefore really the personal reign of Christ in the heart of every one who accepts him. The conquest is slow – that is, the heavenly King finds his kingdom under alien sway, and to get full possession and to reign supreme and alone he must subdue the whole of the old nature. It is this work of conquest and subjugation that goes on in this world, and it is not complete until the believer passes into heaven. All earthly Christian life is therefore a learning to be a Christian. We should bend all the energies of our being toward the bringing of heart, mind, and will into complete subjection to our King.

April 27

UPLIFTING POWER

Has Christ's friendship been to you as close, personal, tender, constant, as the human friendships that have been dearest? The close friends of Christ have found no other influence so strong as his precious friendship in forming and transforming their lives. Continually before them in all its purity and spotlessness, in all its strength and heroism, in all its gentleness and beauty, that fair life has shone, a pattern in the mount let down from heaven for mortals to fashion their lives upon, brought down close to them and winning them by its loveliness. No one who has had Christ for friend in any true, real sense has failed to be blessed by him in the way of growth into nobler, richer life.

April 28

IMMORTAL WORK

Nothing done in matter is immortal, for matter is perishable. The noblest monument of earthly builder will crumble; but he who works on the unseen, the spiritual, leaves impressions that shall endure for ever. The touch of beauty you put upon a life yesterday by the earnest words you spoke, by the new impulse you started in the heart of your friend, by the vision of heavenly purity you gave in your own life to one who was with you, will be bright when suns and stars shall have burned out to blackness. What we do on immortal lives is immortal. He is wise, therefore, who chooses to do his life's work on materials that shall never perish. Thousand of years hence he will find the things he has done enduring still in immortal beauty.

April 29

WORLDLY MOTIVE IN CHRISTIAN LIFE

There is a great deal of worldly policy and prudence in the Christian Church. There are those who shrink from duties through timidity or fear of the consequences. There are those who are restrained from taking the right side of important questions, or boldly declaring their beliefs, through motives of practical expediency. Too many professing Christians lack courage to speak to others about their spiritual interests, fearing rebuff. The money question, it must be confessed, weighs sometimes in the balance in the shaping of the course of Christian men, the decision turning on the answer to the question, 'What will be the effect of this or that course on my business or on my social standing?' We all know well that such worldly policy ought to have no place among the motives that sway the minds of Christian people The only desire should be to know what is right, what is duty, what is the will of God. To be swayed by any other influence is to be unfaithful to our Lord.

April 30

NEED OF RESERVE

Many a great battle turns at last on the reserve. The struggle is perfectly balanced, and victory is uncertain. Then one side or the other brings up its reserve, and instantly the question is settled. Life's battles and crises are determined in like manner, ofttimes, by the reserve or the absence of reserve. No life is a dead level of experience from cradle to grave.

The days are not all bright. The course is not all smooth. The experiences are not all easy. We must all be assailed by temptations and by spiritual foes, when victory can be gained only if we have reserves of resistance to call into action. We must all stand before tasks and duties which will altogether baffle our ability if we have no more strength to draw on than we have been using in the common duties of the common days. Blessed are they who have learned to draw on the infinite resources of divine strength; with the fulness of God as reserve they can never fail.

MAY

May 1

THE LAW OF MINISTRY

God sets before us work, conflict, self-denial, cross-bearing. The central law of Christian life is ministry, serving. You quote, 'Man's chief end is to glorify God and to enjoy him for ever.' Yes; but there is no way of glorifying God save by living to bless the world in Christ's name, to bless men by serving them, loving them, helping them, doing them good. We are debtor, therefore, to every man we meet. We owe him love; we owe him service. We are not to set ourselves up on little thrones and demand homage and service from others; rather *we* are to do the serving. Christ came 'not to be ministered unto, but to minister,' and we should be as our Lord.

May 2

UNSPOKEN PRAYER

Every thought that flies through your brain is heard in heaven. God hears wishes, heart-longings, aspirations, soul-hungerings and thirstings. Do not grieve, then, if you cannot find words in which to tell God what you want, if you cannot put into well-defined thoughts the hopes and hungers of your heart. When words and even thoughts fail, pray in silent yearnings, in unutterable longings, and God will understand just as well as if you spoke in common language. Much of our best praying is done when we sit at God's feet and do not speak at all, but only let our hearts talk.

> 'Rather, as friends sit sometimes, hand in hand,
> Nor mar with words the sweet speech of their eyes,
> So in soft silence let us oftener bow,
> Nor try with words to make God understand.
> Longing is prayer; upon its wings we rise
> To where the breath of heaven beats upon our brow.'

May 3

CHRISTIAN LOVE

The spirit of Christian love, if allowed to work deeply and thoroughly in all hearts and lives, will prevent variance and alienation among Christians. It will lead us to forget ourselves and think of others, not pushing our own interests unduly nor demanding the first place, but in honour preferring one another. It will make us willing to serve, to minister, even to stoop down to unloose a brother's shoes. It will make us thoughtful, too, in all our acts, in our manners, in our words. It will make us gentle, kindly, patient, teaching us to be all what Christ would be if he were in our place.

May 4

THE LIFE THAT WINS

We can win others to Christ only by being Christ to them, by showing them Christ is ourselves, by living so that they may be attracted to Christ, and may learn to admire and to love him by what they see of him in us. One of the most effective ways of winning souls is through beautiful, gentle, Christ-like living. Eloquence of persuasion in a preacher is powerful with sinners only in so far as the preacher's life is consistent. Preaching without love in the life is only empty clatter. But where deep, true love, the love of Christ, is, the plainest, humblest words become eloquent and mighty.

May 5

RECOGNITION IN HEAVEN

is the Father's house. A father's house is a home; and can you think for one moment of a home in which the members of the household do not know each other? The sweetest, best, happiest, and most perfect earthly home is but a dim picture of the love and gladness of the home in heaven. Heaven is like a holy home, only infinitely sweeter, truer and better. Home has been called 'heaven's fallen sister'. If in the imperfect homes of this world we find so much gladness in the ties that bind heart to heart and knit life to life, may we not be confident that in the perfect home of our heavenly Father all this gladness will be infinitely deepened and enriched? Love will not be different in heaven; it will be wondrously purified and exalted, but earthly love will live on through death into eternity.

May 6

OBEDIENCE IN HEAVEN

Obedience makes heaven. All the life of heaven is simply perfect obedience. A little of heaven comes into our life on earth when we learn to obey the will of God. Obedience is the mark of royalty. Wherever God finds a soul that is ready to yield always to his will, to do his commandments without question, to submit to his providences without murmuring, there is a life that he is ready to crown. We get to be like Christ just as we learn to obey and do God's will. Heaven comes down into our heart just as we yield our lives to God.

May 7

WHY SO CHARY OF KINDNESS?

We let our friends go through life without many marks of appreciation. We are chary of compliments. We hide our tender interest and our kindly feelings. We are afraid to give each other the word of praise or of encouragement lest we should seem to flatter, lest we should turn each other's head. Even in many of our homes there is a strange dearth of good, whole-hearted, cheering words. Let us not be afraid to say appreciative and complimentary words when they are deserved and are sincere. Let us lose no opportunity to show kindnesses, to manifest sympathy, to give encouragement. Silence in the presence of needs that words would fill is sinful.

May 8

ROOM IN A HUMBLE SPHERE

When you are tempted to chafe and repine at the narrowness of your circumstances and the limitations of your sphere, remember that Jesus, with all his rich life and all his great powers, for thirty years found room in a humble peasant home for worthy living and for service not unfitted to his exalted character. If you can do nothing but live a true Christian life – patient, gentle, kindly, pure – in your home, in society, at your daily duty, you will perform in the end a service of great value and leave many blessings in the world. Such a life is a little gospel, telling in sermons without words the wonderful story of the cross of Christ.

May 9

LOVE'S SUPREME MOMENTS

Love in its supreme moments does not stop at a little. It does not weigh and measure and calculate and restrain its impulses and check its floods. They know nothing of love who think strange of Mary's costly deed, who try to explain why she acted so prodigally, so lavishly, so wastefully, when she put upon her Lord the highest honour she could bestow upon him. If our love for Christ were only stronger, deeper, richer, we would not need to have Mary's deed explained; we would not calculate so closely how much we can afford to give or do.

May 10

THE PERIL OF FAILURE

Myriads of lives with magnificent possibilities have been utter failures because men and women have not gone promptly to duty at the divine call. They were intended to fill certain places. God made them for these places and qualified them for them; but when they were summoned to their work they excused themselves on one plea or another, and buried their talents in the earth. Let us train ourselves to obey every call of God, lest in our hesitancy, distrust, or disobedience we fail of the mission for which we were made, and meet the doom of the useless in God's universe.

May 11

IF WE KNEW

We should learn to look at the faults of others only through love's eyes, with charity, patience and compassion. We do not know the secret history of the lives of others about us. We do not know what piercing sorrows have produced the scars which we see in people's souls. We do not know the pains and trials which make life hard to many with whom we are tempted to be impatient. If we knew all the secret burdens and the heart-wounds which many carry hidden beneath their smiling faces, we would be patient and gentle with all men.

May 12

THE SECRET OF PEACE

Perfect loyalty to Christ brings perfect peace into the heart. The secret of Christ's own peace was his absolute devotion to his Father's will. We can find peace in no other way. Any resistance to God's will, any disobedience of his law, any wrenching of our lives out of his hand, must break the peace of our hearts. No lesson that he gives ever mars our peace if we receive it with willing, teachable spirit, and strive to learn it just as he has written it out for us. If we take the lessons just as our Master gives them to us, we shall make our life all music, and we shall find peace.

May 13

PRAYER IN SORROW

'Being in an agony, he prayed,' is the record of our Saviour's Gethsemane experience. The lesson stands for all time. Like a bright lamp the little sentence shines amid the olive trees of the garden. It shows us the path to comfort in our time of sorrow. Never before or since was there such grief as the Redeemer's that night, but in his prayer he found comfort. As we watch him the hour through, we see the agony changing as he prayed, until at last its bitterness was all gone, and sweet, blessed peace took its place. The gate of prayer is always the gate to comfort. There is no other place to go. We may learn also from our Lord's Gethsemane how to pray in our Gethsemanes. God will never blame us for asking to have the cup removed nor for the intensity of our supplication; but we must always pray with submission. It is when we say, in our deepest intensity, 'Not my will, but thine,' that comfort comes, that peace comes.

May 14

GOD'S STRANGE SCHOOLS

No books, no universities, can teach us the divine art of sympathy. We must be sorely tempted ourselves before we can understand what others suffer in their temptations. We must have sorrow ourselves in some form before we can be real and true comforters of others in their times of sorrow. We must walk through the deep valley ourselves before we can be guides to others in the same shadowy vales. We must feel the strain and carry the burden and endure the struggle ourselves, and then we can be touched with the feeling of sympathy or can give help to others in life's sore stress and poignant need. So we see one compensation of suffering: it fits us for being in a larger sense helpers of others.

May 15

THE LARGENESS OF DUTY

Duty is always too great for earnest souls. No one can do all that he knows he ought to do or that he wants to do. When we have done our duty, however, day by day, faithfully and earnestly, according to the light and the wisdom given to us at the time, it ought not to cause us regret afterward if it appear that we might have done it with more wisdom or with greater skill. We cannot get the benefits of experience until we have had the experience. We cannot have manhood's ripe wisdom in the days of your youth. We can always see when a day is done how we might have lived it better. We should bring to every hour's work our finest skill, our best wisdom, our purest strength, and then feel no regret even if it does not seem well done. Perfection is ever an unreached goal in this life. Duty is always too large for us to do more than a fragment of it.

May 16

THE TEST OF AMUSEMENTS

Is the love of pleasure growing upon you, gaining the power and the ascendency over you? Is it dulling the keenness of your zest for spiritual pleasures? Is it making Bible-study, prayer, communion with Christ, meditation upon holy themes, less sweet enjoyments than before? Is it making your hunger for righteousness, for God, less intense? Is it interfering with the comfort and blessing you used to find in church services, in Christian work? If so, there is only one thing to do – to hasten to return to God, to cut off the pleasures that is imperilling the soul, and to find in Christ the joy which the world cannot give and which never harms the life. We must test all our pleasures by this rule: Are they helping us to grow into the noblest spiritual beauty?

May 17

LIVING TO SERVE

True life, wherever it is found, is ministry. Men think that they rise in life as they get away from serving; but it is the reverse. 'Not to be ministered unto, but to minister,' our Lord gave as the central aim and desires of his life. These words give us also the ideal for all Christian life. The whole of Christ's wonderful biography is focused and printed here. He himself holds up the picture as the pattern on which every disciple's life is to be fashioned. No one really begins to live at all in any worthy sense until selfishness dies in him and he begins to serve. We should ourselves ask concerning others not how we can use them to advance our interests and our welfare, but how we can do them good, serve them, become in some way blessings to them.

May 18

MAKING AND KEEPING FRIENDS

It is worth while to make friends if they are worthy. It costs to do it; we can have friends only by giving our life for them and to them. Selfishness never wins a friend. We can make others love us only by truly loving them. The largest service, if we do not love, wins us no real friends. Then the friends we have made we should grapple with hooks of steel and keep for ever. No friendship should be formed which is not beautiful enough for heaven. God will never be jealous of the pure human affections we have in glory. Even the brightness of Christ's radiance will not eclipse for our eyes the faces of the earthly friends we shall meet on the golden streets. Loving God supremely will not drive out of our hearts the love of dear ones knit to us along the years of fellowship in joy and sorrow. The better we love Christ, the deeper, purer, tenderer and stronger will be our love for Christly human friends.

May 19

WEAVING OUR SOUL'S GARMENTS

We are all busy weavers. For ever are we throwing the shuttle backward and forward, each moment leaving one new thread in the web of our life which shall stay there for ever. Every thought, every feeling, every motion, every light fancy that plays but for a moment in the soul, becomes a thread which is instantly a permanent part of the life we are living. Our words and acts are threads clean and beautiful or stained and blemished, according to their moral character. Thus we are for ever weaving, and the web that we make our souls must wear in eternity. How important it is that we put into this fabric only threads of immortal beauty! If we do God's will always, and train ourselves to think over God's thoughts, and to receive into our hearts the influences of God's love and grace, and to yield ever and only to God's Spirit, we shall weave for our souls a seamless robe of righteous which shall appear radiant and lovely when all earth's garments have faded and crumbled to dust.

May 20

LIFE'S REAL PROBLEM

The problem of sailing is not to keep the vessel out of the water, but to keep the water out of the vessel. In like manner, the problem of true Christian living is not to keep ourselves out of life's cares, trials and temptations, but to keep the cares, trials and temptations out of us. As the sea is the normal element for ship-sailing, so care is the normal element of life in this world. But we must keep the sea out of our heart. Some people make the mistake of letting their cares and worries creep into their souls. The result is that they grow discontented, fretful, unhappy. The secret of peace is to keep the heart free from care and anxiety even in the midst of the sorest trials. This secret we can have only by opening our hearts to Christ.

May 21

NOT IN VAIN IN THE LORD

We must not measure by an earthly standard in testing the failure or success of life. There are lives which the world crowns as successful, but which Heaven rates as failures. Then there are others over which men drop a tear of pity, but which in God's sight are put down as noble successes. All earnest Christians do many things which they hope will prove blessings to others, which yet in the end seem to fail altogether of good result. But we do not know what good may yet come out of our true work that has appeared to fail. 'Your labour is not in vain in the Lord.' It may not show any result at once, but somewhere, sometime, there will be blessing from everything that is done truly for Christ. The old water-wheel runs around and around outside the mill. It seems to be accomplishing nothing, but the shaft goes through the wall and turns machinery inside, making flour to feed the hunger of many or driving spindles and weaving beautiful fabrics. Our lives may seem, with all their activities, to be leaving no result, but they reach into the unseen; and who knows what blessings they become, what impressions they leave on other lives and in eternity?

May 22

DOING GOD'S WILL

Doing God's will builds up character in us. Doing God's will builds up in us that which shall never need to be torn down. 'He that doeth the will of God abideth for ever.' Every obedience of our lives adds a new touch of beauty on our soul. Every true thing we do in Christ's name, though it leave no mark anywhere else in God's universe, leaves an imperishable mark on our own life. Every deed of kindness or unselfishness that we perform, with love in our hearts for Christ, though it bless no other soul in all the wide world, leaves its benediction on ourselves. We are sure, therefore, or getting a blessing in our own life when we are obedient, even though we impart no good to any other.

May 23

GIVING TO BEGGARS

To the blind man begging by the wayside, to the poor wretch that comes to our door for alms, to the crippled old woman who sits muffled up on a doorstep and holds out a wrinkled hand, we owe something if we are Christians. We may not give money – usually we had better not give money – but we ought to give something. We represent Christ in this world, and we ought to treat every such case of need and misfortune as our Master would do if he were precisely in our place. We ought to give at least a patient answer, a kindly look, and sympathetic attention. This from Turgeneff's 'Poems in Prose': 'I was walking in the street; a beggar stopped me – a frail old man. His tearful eyes, blue lips, rough rags, disgusting sores, – oh, how horribly poverty had disfigured the unhappy creature! He stretched out to me his red, swollen, filthy hand; he groaned and whimpered for alms. I felt in all my pockets. No purse, watch or handkerchief did I find. I had left them all at home. The beggar waited, and his outstretched hand twitched and trembled slightly. Embarrassed and confused, I seized his dirty hand and pressed it: "Don't be vexed with me, brother! I have nothing with me, brother." The beggar raised his bloodshot eyes to mine, his blue lips smiled, and he returned the pressure of my chilled fingers. "Never mind, brother,' stammered he; 'I thank you for this; this too was a gift, brother." I felt that I too had received a gift from my brother.' The brotherly word was holiest alms.

May 24

HOW TO KNOW CHRIST

To some Christ is a creed and a pattern of life, but not a personal friend. There are many who know well the 'historic Christ' but to whom he is only a person who lived nearly two thousand years ago. They read his biography as they read that of St. Paul or St. John, admiring and wondering, and ofttimes saying, in the lines of the children's hymn:

'I wish that His hands had been placed on my head,
    That his arms had been thrown around me,
And that I might have seen his kind look when he said,
    "Let the little ones come unto me.'

They think of his sweet life as but a vanished dream; or, if they realize his resurrection, he is to them an absent friend, like a dear one journeying in another land – real, loving, true, trusted, but far away. But all such miss the sweetest blessedness of knowing Christ. He does not belong to the past nor to the far away, but is a friend who would come into the actual daily life of each of his believing ones. No mother was ever so much to her child as Jesus would be to us if we would let him into our life. How can we get this blessing of personal knowledge of Christ and conscious personal friendship with him? Trust him and obey him, and you will learn you know him and love him.

May 25

NOTHING GOOD COMES EASILY

Unselfishness, even in its smallest acts and manifestations, costs some sacrifice. Work for others which costs us nothing is scarcely worth doing. It takes heart's blood to heal hearts. It is those who sow in tears that shall reap in joy. Take easy work if you will, work that costs you nothing, give only what you will not miss, spare yourself from self-denial and waste and sacrifice; but be not surprised if your hands are empty in the harvest-time. We must give if we are to receive; we must sow if we would reap.

May 26

GOD'S STOREHOUSES

Each step in the life of faith is toward richer blessing. Are you God's child? There is nothing before you in the unopened future but goodness. Every new experience, whether of joy or sorrow, will be a new storehouse of goodness for you. Even in the heart of disaster you will still find goodness infolded. Even your disappointments will disclose truer, richer, blessings than if your own hopes had been realized. Here is a lens through which every true Christian may see his own path clear to the end – from goodness to richer goodness, from glory to glory, the last step through the opening door of heaven into the presence of the King.

May 27

BRUISED REEDS

Christ is building his kingdom with earth's broken things. Men want only the strong, the successful, the victorious, the unbroken, in building their kingdoms; but God is the God of the unsuccessful, of those who have failed. Heaven is filling with earth's broken lives, and there is no bruised reed that Christ cannot take and restore to glorious blessedness and beauty. He can take the life crushed by pain or sorrow and make it into a harp whose music shall be all praise. He can lift earth's saddest failure up to heaven's glory.

May 28

OPPOSITION A MEANS OF GRACE

Spiritual life needs opposition to bring out its best development. It flourishes most luxuriantly in adverse circumstances. The very temptations which make our life one unceasing warfare train us into true soldiers of Christ. The hardnesses of our experiences, which seem to us to be more than we can possibly endure, make the very school of life for us in which we learn our best lessons and grow into whatever beauty and Christlikeness of character we attain.

May 29

LIFE'S POSSIBILITIES

Think of all the magnificent powers God has put into these lives of ours. He has given us minds to think, to reason, to imagine, to roam amid the stars, to wander into the very borders of infinity, to climb the golden stairs of faith even into the midst of heaven's brightness. He has given us hearts to feel, to suffer, to rejoice, to love. He has put into our beings the possibilities of the noblest achievements and the loftiest attainments. Oh, what a shame it is for one born to live in immortal glory, called to be a child of God, to become like the Son of God, yet to be content with a poor earthly life, and to live without reaching up toward God and heaven!

May 30

OUR SOLDIERS' GRAVES

We do not always remember, as we enjoy our national blessings and comforts, that they cost those who won them for us, and those who have conserved them and passed them down to us. We strew flowers on the graves of our soldiers who fell, and tell in song and speech of their heroic deeds. This is well. We should never let the gratitude die out of our hearts as we think of the blood that was shed in saving our country. But gratitude is not enough. This redeemed country is a sacred trust in our hands. We are now the conservators of its glory. We have more to do than sing the praises of its dead heroes and soldiers. There are battles yet to fight – battles for national honour, for righteousness, for truth, for purity, for religion. We must hold up the old fag in the face of all enemies. While we honour the memory of those who died in patriotic and holy war, let us ourselves be worthy soldiers in the great moral war that never ceases, and patriots loving country more than party, and truth and righteousness more than political preferment and reward.

May 31

MASTERING MISFORTUNE

An English prisoner, suffering from persecution, was cheered for one hour each day by a little spot of sunshine on his dungeon-wall. Through a grating high up the sun's rays streamed down into his cell for this little time. He found on his floor an old nail and a stone, and with these rude implements he cut upon the wall while the sunlight lay there a rough image of the Christ upon his cross. Thus he mastered his misfortune, getting blessing out of it. The incident has its lesson for us all. Whatever the calamity or the disaster that builds its dungeon-walls about you, never let despair lay its chilly hand upon you. Never yield to the gloom. Never let the darkness into your soul. There is no dungeon so deep and dark but down into its chilling gloom the rays of God's love stream. In the light of these fashion some new beauty on your soul. Carve on the wall of your heart the image of the Christ. Master your misfortune, and make it yield blessing to you. Conquered calamity becomes your helper, and leaves beauty on your soul; but let your trouble master you, and it leaves an ineffaceable scar upon your life.

JUNE

June 1

BEAUTIES OF NATURE

They miss many a tender joy who do not always hold their hearts in sympathy with nature. They lose many a whisper of love that drops from God's lips who have not ears open to catch the voices of nature. They fail to behold many a lovely vision of beauty who have not learned to use their eyes in admiring the exquisite things that God has scattered everywhere in such glorious profusion. Yet most of us walk amid these inspirations, these rare pictures, these sweet voices, and neither feel nor see nor hear. God never meant us to get so little comfort or joy from the lovely things with which he has filled our earth.

June 2

FAILING IN OUR LITTLE PART

God is not so limited in his resources of power that if one little human hand somewhere fails to do its appointed duty his great cause will be defeated. He has large plans, in which the humblest of us have our own allotted place and part. But there is no compulsion brought to bear upon us. We can refuse to do our little piece of work if we choose. God's plan will then go on without us, and other hands will do what we refuse to do. The only effect of our failure in the duty assigned us will be in ourselves. Our own hearts will be hurt by our failure in duty, and we shall be set aside, missing the honour and blessing which would have been ours had we done our part.

June 3

LEAVING ALL TO GOD

As we go through life we learn more and more to doubt our own wishing and choosing, as we see how little really comes from our own ways and plans. We learn not to choose at all ourselves, but to let God choose for us. No doubt we miss heavenly blessings many a time, because we have not faith to take them in their disguise of pain or grief, preferring our own way to our Father's. Then God sometimes lets us have what in our wilfulness we persist in choosing, just to teach us that our own way is not the best. We learn at last to plead, 'Bless me, my Father', not daring to indicate in what manner the blessing shall come, but preferring that it shall be as God wills.

June 4

'AS WE FORGIVE'

We ought to keep no count of offences and forgivenesses, and the time never ought to come when we shall say we can forgive one no more. When we are smarting under some injury done us by another, and when our feeling of resentment is burning into a flame within us, we should remember that the wrong we have done to God is infinitely greater, and that he in his love has freely forgiven us. Should we not, then, be willing to forgive others their little wrongs against us? This is why our Lord put into the prayer he taught his disciples the words, 'Forgive us our debts, as we forgive.' He wants us always to remember that we ourselves need forgiveness, and that if we would be like him we must forgive as he does.

June 5

THE BLESSING OF ASSURANCE

Every Christian's privilege is to enjoy unbroken assurance while living close to Christ. God wants us to trust him just as fully in the shadow as in the sunshine. There is grace enough in Christ to give light and joy in the darkest experience. Yet it is just as true that many of God's noblest saints, in all ages, have had seasons of depression, when they lost the joy of salvation, and could not speak triumphantly of their hope. It is true, also, that there have been many devoted followers of Christ who never in their life could get farther than to hope they were Christ's disciples. Is this the best that the love of God and the grace of Christ can do for those who are saved?

June 6

'I AM READY'

Whatever command God gives, we should instantly and cheerfully answer, 'Yes, Lord; I am ready to obey.' It is not hard to say 'Yes' when God leads us only in easy paths, where the flowers are strewn, where the way is smooth and agreeable. But sometimes the path is covered with thorns, and is rough and steep, or is through fire or flood; still we are always to say, 'Yes'. If it is to some trial or cross-bearing or sacrifice that God calls us, our answer should ever be the same. We ought to be able to trust him when our eyes can see no blessing or good in the way he would take us. Every path of God leads to a rich joy.

June 7

CHOICE OF FRIENDS

We should choose friends whom we can take into every part of our life, into every closest communion, into every holy joy of our heart, into every consecration and service, into every hope, and between whom and us there shall never be a point at which we shall not be in sympathy. We ought to accept only the friendship that will brings blessing to our lives, that will enrich our character, that will stimulate us to better and holier things, that will weave threads of silver and gold into our web of life, whose every influence will be a lasting benediction.

June 8

LIFE'S OPPORTUNITIES

All the days come to us filled with opportunities. There are opportunities for gathering knowledge and for growing wise. There are opportunities for growing in character, becoming stronger, truer, purer, nobler, more Christ-like. There are opportunities for doing heroic things for Christ. There are opportunities for performing gentle ministries and for rendering sweet services in Christ's name to those who need loving sympathy and deeds of kindness. Opportunities come to all – come continually, on all the common days, and come ofttimes in the simplest common things. The trouble with too many of us is that we do not improve them, do not seize them as they pass.

June 9

VICTORY BY STANDING

One of the first things in military training is to learn to stand well. Old soldiers will tell you that there is nothing which so tests the courage and the obedience of men as to be required to stand still on the field and hold a position in the face of the enemy. Ofttime the battles depends upon standing firm. The same principle applies in all life. Much of Christian duty is not active, bustling work, but quiet, patient waiting. There come many times in the experience of every life when victory can be gained in no other way. We must stand still and wait for God. Immeasurable harm is wrought in personal lives and in the work of God by the impatience that cannot wait for the divine bidding to go forward.

June 10

POWER OF THE TONGUE

The tongue's power of blessing is simply incalculable. It can impart valuable knowledge, making others wiser. It can utter kindly sentences that will comfort sorrow or cheer despondency. It can breathe thoughts that will arouse, inspire, and quicken heedless souls, and even call up dead souls to life. It can sing songs which will live for ever in blessed influence and ministry. Such power we should consecrate to God and hold ever pure for him. The lips that speak God's name in prayer and Christian song, and that utter vows of fidelity to Christ, should never defile themselves with any forms of corrupt speech. They should be kept only for Christ.

June 11

INDIVIDUALITY OF CHARACTER

Character is personal. It is not a possession we can share with another. We can give a hungry man part of our loaf of bread; we can divide our money with one who needs; but character is something that we cannot give away or communicate. The brave soldier cannot share his courage with the pale, trembling recruit who fights by his side in the battle. The pure, gentle woman cannot give part of her purity and gentleness to the defiled and hardened sister-woman whom she meets. Character is our own, a part of our very being. It grows in us along the years. Acts repeated become habits, and character is made up in the end of the habits which have been repeated so often as to become a permanent part of the life.

June 12

WORK FOR OTHERS

We can do our best work always when we do it not for ourselves, but that it may bless others. If the motive in all ambition, all toil, all effort, is to become wiser, stronger, greater, more influential, in order that we may do more in Christ's name for our fellow-men, then whatever we do will be beautiful and noble. The motive exalts and ennobles the work. We get the largest measure of good for ourselves from what we do when our first aim is to do good to another. If you would get the best from any good thing, receive it from God and then hasten to minister it in Christ's name to others. The richest blessing comes not in the receiving, but in the giving and doing.

June 13

SECOND-HAND BIBLE TRUTHS

Many Christians have their heads stored full of catechism, creed and Scripture, and yet when trouble comes they have not one truth on which they can really lean or trust their weight, or which gives them any actual support or help. Piles of doctrines, but no rod and staff to lean on in weakness; lamps hung away in great clusters, but not one of them burning to throw its light upon the darkness; bundles of alpenstocks tied up in creed and text, but no staff to walk with over the dark mountains. Let us learn to study the Scriptures for ourselves, and to know what we should believe and why we should believe it. Second-hand Bible truth is not the kind of food our souls need.

June 14

MISREADING PROVIDENCES

We are all apt to interpret 'providences' in accordance with our own desires. When we are wishing to be led in a certain way, we are quite sure to find 'providences' that seem to favour our own preference. We must be careful in interpreting the meaning of events and occurrences. We are not to enter every door that is thrown open before us. The devil opens doors of temptation, but we are not to call opportunities to sin guiding 'providences'. God's voice in providence never contradicts the voice of his word.

June 15

KEEPING A CHILD'S HEART

We ought to keep our hearts warm and full of kindliness and sweet humanness, even through the harshest experiences. Many of us find life hard and full of pain. We meet misfortunes, sore trials, disappointments. We should not allow these harsh experiences to deaden our sensibilities or make us stoical or sour. Nothing but the love of God shed abroad in us by the Holy Spirit can keep any of us in such gentleness and tenderness amid the stern and severe experiences of life. Yet it is possible to carry the gentle heart of a little child through all life's hardness and chill into the fullest and ripest old age.

June 16

SETTING PAIN TO MUSIC

In 'Marble Faun,' Miriam, the broken-hearted singer, puts into a burst of song the pent-up grief of her soul. This was better, surely, than if she had let it forth in a wild shriek of pain. The religion of Christ would teach us to put into song every anguish and all sorrow. It would set to music our deepest, saddest experiences. It would have us sing even our heart's bitterest plaints. It gives us anthems rather than dirges for the utterance of our sorest griefs. It helps us to do this by revealing to our faith's vision something of beauty and blessing in every dark hour, something other eyes cannot see. It lets us hear in our deepest trials the voices of divine love, encouraging, cheering, assuring us. Surely the lesson is worth the learning. It is nobler to sing a victorious song in time of trial than to lie crushed in grief. Songs bless the world more than wails and tears. They also honour God more. It is better for our own heart, too, to put our sorrows and pains into songs.

June 17

DIVINE DISCONTENT

The ideal Christian life is one of insatiable thirst, of quenchless yearning, of divine discontent, wooed ever on by visions of new life, new joy, new attainments. The trouble with too many of us is that we are too well satisfied with ourselves as we are. We have attained a little measure of peace, of holiness, of faith, of joy, of knowledge of Christ, and we are not hungering for the larger possible attainments. O pray for discontent! With all the infinite possibilities of spiritual life before you, do not settle down on a little patch of dusty ground at the mountain's foot in restful content. Be not content till you reach the mountain's summit.

June 18

THE POWER OF FAITH

God can use very weak and imperfect agents. He can do great things with poor instruments. But there is one kind of person he will not use. He will not send blessing to the world through an unbelieving heart. If you would be a vessel meet for the Master's use, you must have faith. Believe in Christ. Believe that he is able and willing to do the 'greater things' which he has promised to do through his disciples. Open your heart to receive him and all that he brings. Expect him to do great things through you. If we have faith, there is no limit to what Christ will do for us. Faith lays our powers in Christ's hands, as the chisel lays itself in the hands of the sculptor for the carving of the marble statue.

June 19

BLESSED ARE THE PEACEMAKERS

There are causes enough to separate people and to produce frictions and alienations. Let us not add to the world's bitterness and grief by ever encouraging strife or putting a single coal on the fire of anger. Rather let us try to heal the little rifts we find in people's friendships. The unkind thoughts of another we find in any one's mind let us seek to change to kindly thoughts. We can do no more Christ-like service in this world than habitually and continually to seek to promote peace between man and man, to keep people from drifting apart, and to draw friends and neighbours closer together in love.

June 20

'WHATSOEVER THINGS ARE LOVELY'

We become truly beautiful just in the measure that we become like God. Human holiness is not always beautiful. There are men who are good but not lovely. They have qualities that repel others. But true holiness is attractive. We ought to make our religion so beautiful that all who look upon us shall be drawn to our Master. We do dishonour to Christ when we profess to be his people, and yet show in our character, disposition, and life things that are unlike Christ. How will men of the world know what true religion is if you and I do not show them its beauty in our lives? We should seek not only whatsoever things are just and true and honest, but also whatsoever things are lovely.

June 21

LOVE FOR THE BRETHREN

It is easy enough to love some people – people with tastes
like ours, people who belong to our 'set', people who are
particularly kind to us. But that is not the way Christ wants
us to live and to love. True Christian fellowship takes in all
the followers of our Lord, all who bear his name. We are to
be known as disciples by our love for one another. It requires
grace to love all Christians. We must have the love of God
in our hearts before we can do it. We must be close to Christ
before we can be close to each other. We must cultivate the
thoughts and feelings of the brotherhood that is in Christ.
The humblest believer is our brother, because he is a
Christian. We are one in Christ.

June 22

BETWEEN THEE AND HIM ALONE

Let us learn to seal our lips for ever on the wretched,
miserable habit of telling the world about the motes in our
neighbour's eye. Who made us a judge over him? Tell him
his faults between thee and him alone. You can find chapter
and verse for that. Tell him his faults, if you will, with love
and sympathy in your heart, confessing your own to him
meanwhile. Tell him his faults because you want to help
him to become nobler, lovelier, and better, because you
cannot bear to see a stain upon him, not because you want
to humble him or glory over him. Tell him his faults in secret
if you are ready for such holy work; but do not, do not tell
the world of his faults.

June 23

CHRIST-LIKENESS AT HOME

Keep the lamp of love shining day after day amid the multitude of home cares and home duties, amid the criticisms of home playfulness and thoughtlessness, amid the thousand little irritations and provocations of home life which so tend to break peace and mar sweet temper. Let home love be of the kind that never faileth. Wherever else, far away or near, you pour the bright beams of your Christian life, be sure you brighten the space close about you in your own home. No goodness and gentleness outside will atone for unlovingness and uncharitableness at home.

June 24

GETTING READY FOR TEMPTATION

We must all meet temptation, and the tempter comes so suddenly and so insidiously that if we cannot instantly repel his assaults we shall be foiled. There is nothing like texts of Scripture to drive Satan away. We need to have our quiver full of these polished shafts, these invincible darts, and to keep them ever ready to draw out on a moment's notice to hurl at our enemy. The only way to do this is to make the Word of God our daily study, storing in our memory its precious texts, its counsels, its promises, its warnings. Then we shall never be surprised, unprepared or defenceless, but for every temptation shall have a dart ready to draw out and hurl at our adversary.

June 25

THE LOVE OF CHRIST

God puts something of himself into every true human life. He helps and blesses us through our friendships, but these are meant only to help us up to himself. Christ Jesus is the only man in whom we may have eternal trust. All other friendships are but fragments; his is the perfect friendship. Behind the sweet, gentle humanities in him, which make it so easy for us to come to him and repose in him, is the might of the eternal God. When we come to this precious human love, for which our hearts crave, and which seems so satisfying, we know that infinite divine fulness lies behind the tender warmth. The humanity comes very close to us, and it is for us to lay our heads upon its bosom. Then when we lean on him we are lifted up in the arms of Omnipotence.

June 26

WHATSOEVER THY HAND FINDETH

Find your work wherever Christ has put you. Do whatever he gives you to do. Strive to be full of Christ; then strive to be Christ to the souls about you that are lost and perishing or that are in need or sorrow. Seek to make one little spot of this world brighter, better, purer. Christ has redeemed you and lifted you up, that you may redeem and lift up others about you. If your hand is only ready for service, you will always find work ready for your hand.

June 27

DOING GOD'S WILL

We are never to be rebellious or slow to submit to God, but we must be sure that we have done all we can before we fold our hands and say, 'Thy will be done.' There come many experiences, however, in which we can do nothing, and can only submit. We must not only ourselves strive faithfully in all things to do the will of God, but must suffer it to be done in us, even when it lays us low in the dust, even when it strips us bare and shatters all our joys. This will is to be accepted, too, not rebelliously, with murmuring and complaint, but songfully, joyfully, lovingly.

June 28

CREED AND LIFE

'It makes small difference what a man believes, what doctrines he holds: it is conduct that counts.' That is the way some people talk as they fling their flippant sneers at creeds. But it does matter what one believes. Wrong believing leads to wrong living. The heathen who worships a god that he conceives of as lustful, cruel and unholy becomes himself lustful, cruel and unholy. The Christian who worships a God who is revealed to him as holy, righteous, pure and good, becomes himself holy, righteous, pure and good. Thus beliefs shape the life. It is important, therefore, that we know the truths about the character and will of Christ, as our conception of Christ will print itself upon our life.

June 29

FINDING THE GOOD IN GOD'S WORLD

Thankfulness or unthankfulness is largely a matter of eyes. Two men look at the same scene: one beholds the defects, the imperfections; the other beholds the beauty, the brightness. If you cannot find things to be thankful for today, every day, the fault is in yourself, and you ought to pray for a new heart, a heart to see God's goodness and to praise him. A happy heart transfigures all the world for us. It finds something to be thankful for in the barest circumstances, even in the night of sorrow. Let us train ourselves to see the beauty and the goodness in God's world, in our own lot, and then we shall stop grumbling, and all our experience shall start songs of praise in our heart.

June 30

NOT YOUR WORK, BUT YOU

It is not so much your work as you that God wants; at least he wants you first, and then your work. Service from hearts that are not really consecrated to God is not pleasing to him. We are in danger of forgetting this in our busy, bustling days. It is easier to offer God a few activities than to give him a heart. The tendency of the religious life at present is to work, to service, rather than to loving God. So we need to remind ourselves continually that loving must come before doing and serving. The largest and most conspicuous work will find no acceptance with God if our hearts are not his.

"'Tis not thy work the Master needs, but thee –
    The obedient spirit, the believing heart,
The child obedient, trustful, glad to be
    Where'ver He will, to stay or to depart.'

JULY

July 1

THE VALUE OF TIME

Our days are like beautiful summer fields as God gives them to us. The minutes are blooming flowers and silvery grass-blades and stalks of wheat with their germs of golden grains. The hours are trees with their rich foliage of vines with their blossom-prophecies of purple clusters. Oh the fair, blessed possibilities of the days and hours and minutes as they come to us from God's hands! But what did you do with yesterday? How does the little acre of that one day look to you now? What are we doing with our time? Every moment God gives us has in it a possibility of beauty as well as something to be accounted for. Are we using our time for God?

July 2

FOR THE SAKE OF CHRIST

Love to Christ must be the spring and inspiration of all duty, all heroism, all fine achievements, all service to our fellow-men. 'In His Name' is the true motto of all Christian living. Serving our fellow-men amounts to nothing in heaven's sight if it is not done for the sake of Christ. The service must be really rendered to Christ, no matter to whom the kindness is shown, or otherwise there is no exaltation in it, however beautiful it may be in itself. Things we do from any other motive have no acceptableness in the sight of God.

July 3

WATCH YOUR HEART-LIFE

We need to watch our heart-life, for it is in thoughts, feelings, dispositions, moods, tempers, affections, that all departure from Christ begins. We need to watch our inner spiritual state. The world may see no abatement in our zeal, in our religious activity, in our earnest advocacy of the truth, and yet there may be less prayerfulness, less love for Christ, less tenderness of conscience, less hunger for righteousness, less desire for holiness. Is Christ more to you now than ever he was before? Does his love constrain you with overmastering sway? Can you say, with Zinzendorf, 'I have only one passion, and that is He'? Is your heart right?

July 4

PRAYING FOR OUR COUNTRY

We need to pray much for our country. Perhaps we err in making our prayers ordinarily only for ourselves and for our own little world. Certainly our country ought to have a place in the daily supplications of every Christian. Those who rule over us ought to be continually remembered. They are men, and need divine wisdom and guidance. They are men under the sway of partisan influence, and we need to pray that they be kept free from any domination which would lead them to forget God. We need to pray for our institutions, that they be kept pure and holy – that righteousness may prevail throughout the land. We need to pray for all our people, that they might be made good citizens – that uprightness and integrity may characterize them. 'Happy is that people whose God is the Lord.'

July 5

OVER-ANSWERED PRAYER

No true, faith-winged prayer goes unanswered, but many a prayer that seems to us unanswered is really over-answered. The very thing we ask God does not grant, because he is able to do something infinitely better for us. We ask only for bodily help or relief, and he sees that we need far more, some deep spiritual blessing. He answers our soul's needs before he gratifies our personal wishes. We ask for a temporal favour; he does not give it to us, but instead he bestows upon us a spiritual good which will enrich us for ever. We ask for the lifting away of a burden or the averting of a sorrow; our plea is not granted in form, but instead we receive a new impartation of the power of Christ, or an angel comes from heaven and ministers to us. Thus many times our little prayers are really over-answered.

July 6

PASS ON YOUR BLESSING

God does not like to bestow his blessings where they will be hoarded, but he loves to put them into the hands of those who will do the most with them to bless their fellows. The central object of true living is to be helpful to others. The true life is one devoted to Christ, to be used then for him in blessing others. Lay every gift at the Master's feet, and then, when it has been blessed by him, carry it out to bless others. Bring your barley loaves to Christ, and then, with the spell of his touch upon them, you may feed hungry thousands with them.

July 7

UNDER GOD'S ORDERS

Wherever God puts us, he has something definite just there for us to do – something which he has brought us there on purpose to do. There is something he created you specially to do. He brings you every day into places where it is true that you are there for a definite duty. Every time we find ourselves in the presence of a need or an opportunity for helpfulness, we may well stop and ask if God has not brought us to this point for this very thing. We are every really under orders. Ofttimes the orders are sealed, and are opened only as the hours move. To realize this gives all our commonest life a sacredness that should make us reverent. We are continually serving our King.

July 8

THE BEGINNINGS OF BITTERNESS

Let us instantly crush the beginning of envy, jealousy and hate in our hearts, never allowing the day to close on a bitter feeling. The hour of evening prayer, when we bow at God's feet, should always be a time for getting right everything that may have gone wrong with us and in us during the day. Then every injury should be forgiven when we pray, 'Forgive us, as we forgive.' Then every spark of envy or jealousy or anger should be quenched, and the love of Christ should be allowed to flood our hearts. We should never allow the sun to go down on our anger.

July 9

WRITTEN NOT WITH INK

The world does not read the Bible nor come to church to hear the minister. All it learns about Christ and the Christian life it must learn from those who bear Christ's name and represent him. If all church-members lived truly consecrated lives – holy, beautiful, separate from the world, loyal to Christ in business, in pleasure, in all things – it is impossible to estimate what the saving power of the Church would be in example alone. It is an awful thought that professing Christians, by the inconsistencies of their personal lives, lead souls to reject the Saviour. We are all responsible for the influence of our example. Our lives should be New Testament pages that all could read.

July 10

GRACE FOR THE DAY

God does not give us his grace as he gives his sunshine – pouring it out on all alike. He discriminates in spiritual blessings. He gives strength according to our need. His eye is ever on us in tender, watchful love, and what we need at the time he supplies. He gives us grace for grace. When one grace is exhausted another is ready. The grace is always timely. It is not given in large store in advance of the need, but is ready always in time. It may not always be what we wish, but it is always what we really want.

July 11

THE TRANSFIGURED LIFE

Holy thoughts in the heart transfigure the life. Your daily thoughts build up your character. Our hearts are the quarries where the blocks are fashioned which we build into our life-temple. If our thoughts and meditations are good, beautiful, true, pure, loving and gentle, our life will grow into Christ-likeness. Professor Drummond tells of a young girl whose character ripened into rare beauty – one of the loveliest lives, he says, that ever bloomed one earth. She always wore about her neck a little locket. But no one was ever allowed to open the locket or to know what it contained. Once, however, in a time of dangerous illness, she permitted a friend to look within it, and there she saw the words, 'Whom having not seen I love.' That was the secret of the dear child's transfiguration of character – loving the unseen Christ. The same love – warm, tender, earnest, glowing in the heart year after year – will transfigure any life into heavenly beauty.

July 12

THE BLESSING OF DOING

It is the building of character that should be our central aim in all life. Business, school, home, church, reading, pleasure, struggle, work, sorrow, all are but means to the one end. I do not care how much money you men made last year; but let me ask earnestly what mark last year's business made upon your character. The growth of one's manhood is of infinitely more importance that the growth of one's fortune. Everything we do leaves its impress within, upon our soul.

We are building life all the while, whatever we are doing. The work itself may fail, but in the worker's disappointment, amid the failure of his plans, the work on his character goes on. Even in defeats the struggling leaves a recompense within. Giving, though nothing good comes from the gift, blesses the giver.

> In the strength of the endeavour,
> In the temper of the giver,
> In the loving of the lover,
>   Lies the hidden recompense.
>
> In the sowing of the sower,
> In the fading of the flower,
> In the fleeting of each hour,
>   Lurks eternal recompense.

July 13

THE INFLUENCE OF WORDS

Words are so easily spoken that we forget what power they have to give pleasure or pain. They seem to vanish so utterly the moment they have dropped from our lips that we forget they do not go away at all, but linger, either like barbed arrows in the heart where they struck or like fragrant flowers distilling perfumes. No matter when we talk with others or on what theme, however playful or light, we should always try to speak some thoughtful word before we part, some word that will give strength or hope or cheer or help. We may not meet our friend again.

July 14

SEEING ONLY THE FAULTS

There are some people who walk through God's fair world, and in the midst of men and women whose lives shine with bright qualities and dazzling gems of character, and yet they have no eyes for any of these radiant beauties. But for every fault and blemish they have the sharpest vision. They judge uncharitably. They think evil where there is none. This is one of the things Christ condemns. We should train ourselves away from a habit of life so unchristian. We should seek to have eyes only for the beauty, not for the blemishes.

July 15

HOME-WORK FOR CHRIST

We are not truly Christians if we are doing nothing for our Lord. But the work of Christ is not all found in the things we do in the Church. Let no one fret who finds no time from love's devoted service for outside or public work for Christ. You are doing most beautiful things for Christ in your unselfish toil, in your sick-room ministry, in your care for your children, in your deeds of kindness to the invalid within your own doors. Only do all in Christ's name, and it will shine like angel's work. Some people God seems to ordain for just such ministry, and to keep ever busy out of the world's sight. Let none such fret that they cannot take part in the public work of the Church.

July 16

PRAYER WITHOUT PROMISE

There are human lives that never learn to sing the songs of faith and peace and love until they enter the darkness of sorrow and trial. Would it be true love for these for God to hear their prayer for the removal of every sorrow and pain? There is no promise for the prayer that God would take out of our life, out of any life, the hindrances, the griefs, the bitternesses. If we pray such a prayer, it must be simply a humble, shrinking request, which we shall refer at once, without undue urging, to the wise and perfect will of God.

July 17

'YE DID IT NOT'

We are too apt to neglect opportunities of helping others and or relieving distress, never thinking that we are sinning against Christ, that we are indeed leaving *him* unhelped and unrelieved when we might have given him sweet comfort. We forget that neglects are sins. 'Ye did it not' is the charge, in our Lord's picture of the Judgment, against those who are bidden to depart. The things we have failed to do will be the things that shall turn the scales on that great trial-day. We must meet our neglects as well as our positive sins.

July 18

VISIONS IN THE WORDS OF CHRIST

Every word of Christ that we ponder deeply opens to us a vision of beauty or excellence – something very lovely, a fragment of Christ's own image – and we should instantly strive to paint the vision on our own life, to get the beauty, the excellence, the loveliness into our own life. Let us learn to be loyal to the word of Christ; not only to know it and ponder it and meditate upon it, but to do it, and to allow it thus to shape and mould our whole being into its own holy beauty. If we hide Christ's words in our hearts, they will transform us into his likeness.

July 19

OUR WEAK HOURS

We are not at all times equally strong. There are days with all of us when we throw off temptation with almost no effort. But none of us are so every day. There are hours with the strongest of us when we are weak. These are the times of peril for us, and our adversary is watching for them. In your weak hours keep a double guard, therefore, against temptation. Keep out of its way. Throw yourself with mighty faith on Him who was tempted in all points as we are, and knows therefore how to deliver us when we are tempted. In time of special weakness run to Christ for shelter.

July 20

INDIVIDUAL RESPONSIBILITY

God looks upon us as individuals. We come into this world one by one. We live in a sense alone with our own personal responsibilities. We die one by one. As individuals, not as crowds, must we stand before God. Your destiny will not depend on any chance of the moment; you are fixing it yourself in your choices and acts, in your habits and life. Your own faith and obedience must weave the garment of beauty for your life. God gives the materials, but after that each one is the weaver of his own 'wedding garment'.

July 21

DOING THINGS FOR CHRIST

We often imagine that it was a great deal easier for our Lord's first disciples to do things for him than it is for us. They could see him and hear his voice and do errands really for him, and coming back hear his approval or his thanks; but we cannot hear him telling us what to do, nor can we see his pleased look when we have done anything for him. So we find ourselves wishing he were here again, that we might get our duties right from his very lips. We sometimes ask how we can do things for him when he is not here. But we have only to remember his promise: 'I am with you all the days.' He is here, though unseen, just as really as he was with his first disciples. We can do things for him all the time. Every loving obedience is something done for Christ. Every kindness shown to another in his name and for his sake is shown to him. Every piece of common, routine task-work, if done through love for him, becomes something done for Christ. So we can make all our dull life radiant as angels ministry by doing all for Christ.

July 22

GOD'S UNCHANGING LOVE

Human love may change. The friendship of last year has grown cold. The gentleness of yesterday has turned to severity. But it is never thus with God's love. It is eternal. Our experience of it may be variable, but there is no variableness in the love. Our lives may change, our consciousness of his love may fade out; but the love clings for ever, the gentleness of God abides eternal. 'For the mountains shall depart, and the hills be removed; but my kindness shall not depart from thee, neither shall the covenant of my peace be removed, saith the Lord that hath mercy on thee.'

July 23

GOD'S PRESENT HELP

There is never a moment, nor any experience, in the life of a true Christian, from the heart of which a message may not instantly be sent up to God, and back to which help may not instantly come. God is not off in some remote heaven merely. He is not away at the top of the long steep life-ladder, looking down upon us in serene calm and watching us as we struggle upward in pain and tears. He is with each one of us on every part of the way. His promise of presence is an eternal present tense – 'I *am* with thee.' So 'Thou God seest me' becomes to the believer a most cheering and inspiring assurance. We are never out of God's sight for a moment. His eye watches each one of us continually, and his heart is in his eye. He comes instantly to our help and deliverance when we are in any need or danger.

July 24

THE GREATEST ATTRIBUTE

The greatest attribute in God is not his power, though it is omnipotence; not his knowledge, though it is omniscience; not his glory, though it is burning majesty: it is his love. He is greatest as he blesses and serves. The brightest hour in Christ's life was not the hour of his transfiguration, or of his miracle-working, or of his sublime teaching, but the hour when he hung in the darkness on his cross. Then it was that his love shone out in the most wondrous revealing. We need to remember for ourselves that the greatest thing in the world is love – that serving is the path to highest honour.

July 25

'OF HIS FULNESS'

Every life will have its times of sore testing, its times of sharp trial, its experiences in which ordinary strength and preparation will not avail. It is when we have Christ behind our own little strength, when we are abiding in Christ, when our faith links us to his everlasting fulness, that we have the reserve we need for any future. True religion binds the soul to God, so that from his divine fulness supply comes for every emergency. We cannot fail if God is behind us. Our lamps can never go out if they are fed from heaven's olive trees. But if we have no such reserve, our own feeble strength will soon be exhausted, and there will be no refilling of the emptied vessel.

July 26

SHRINKING FROM DUTY

When we stand before any duty, whatever peril or cost it may involve, let us not hesitate to do it. You cannot turn away from duty save at the peril of your soul. Forget not the momentous word of Christ: 'Whosoever will save his life shall lose it; but whosoever will lose his life for my sake shall find it.' There are times when the best use we can make of our life is to give it up. Life that is saved by shrinking from duty is not worth saving. It has been stained, and lost its glory in the saving. It is infinitely better to die in the way of duty than to live by cowardice or disloyalty to Christ or by any unfaithfulness.

July 27

AS A FLOWER SCATTERS FRAGRANCE

Stay at Christ's feet till your heart overflows with love for all, even for people you have not liked before. Then begin to think about them and to live for them. Begin to scatter happiness as a flower scatters fragrance, as a lamp scatters beams of light. Christ was always making people happy. Shall we not take the same aim for ours? It is a wonderful power, too – a power that we all have in a greater or smaller measure – to put gladness and joy into others' hearts. No mission in life can be nobler than to live to be a happiness-maker.

July 28

PRAYER AND ANSWER

True prayer is earnest, not tiring nor fainting. It takes every burden to God – the small and the large alike. It is submissive, referring all to the Father's will. Its answer may not come in the direct granting of the request we make, but may come instead in more grace and strength, enabling us to keep the burden and yet rejoice. Lying at our Father's feet in the time of our strong cryings and tears, we learn obedience, and our sobbings end in praises, our struggles in acquiescence, our tears are dried, and we rise victorious – not getting our own way, but glad and happy and peaceful in God's way.

July 29

TAKING SHORT-CUTS

We should never take short-cuts, even to things that we are sure will some day be ours. Life is full of these opportunities to shorten the path to success, to achievement, to position. God's way ofttimes seems long and far around. But any other way, however short it seems, is longer. Though there may be no sin committed in taking the short-cuts, nothing dishonourable done, nothing to stain the soul, still it is better to go only as God leads. His way is always in the end the shortest.

July 30

WHAT WE TRY TO DO

Christ accepts what we try our best to do for him, what we truly want to do, even though no results come from our efforts. This ought to be a comfort to many of us, for we do not do, any of us, indeed, what it is in our hearts to do. Our hands are awkward and unskilful, and fail to work out the beauty that our mind dreams. We go out with high resolve and loving thought to do some sweet service for our Lord, and come back with tears and sad regret over the failure or the marring of what we meant to do. But Christ knows what our hearts planned and what we wanted to do, and *that* is what he counts and sets down on his books.

July 31

BLESSING OF DAILY CROSSES

A true Christian life never grows easy, never becomes entirely agreeable to our natural tastes. Every day is, in a certain sense, a crucifixion, a nailing on the cross. But this very hardness is a means of grace. The cross lifts us upward. We grow under the burden of our daily duties and cares. So it comes that the things we would like to be freed from are the things we could least afford to lose. What we consider our disadvantages may really be our most indispensable advantages. We grow best under pressure, under the hard necessity of toil and care.

AUGUST

August 1

CHRISTIANITY A LIFE

It were easier to get all the sunbeams out of grasses and flowers and plants in the bright summer days than to get the life of Christ out of the world. It has wrought itself into everything along these Christian centuries, not only into the individual lives of Christ's followers, but also into laws and systems and institutions, into thought and literature and music and art. Christianity is not a mere creed. There is that in it which can never be wrapped up in forms, in liturgies, in confessions. Nor is Christianity a mere code of ethics; it is a life, a throbbing, pulsing, immortal life. It enters into men as the sunshine enters into the plant or the flowers. It becomes their very heart's blood, their breath, their spirit. It inspires their thought, their feeling, their words, their acts.

August 2

THE HIDDEN LIFE

We are all conscious of living in this world, even at our best, far below our best. We are conscious, too, of possibilities of character hidden within us undeveloped, and of powers of helpfulness in our life which we have barely begun to exercise, but which might be drawn out into activity. We see hints and gleams, and we have glimpses now and then, of far more glorious life than we have yet reached. The highest attainments here are but the beginnings of sanctified life. The peace, joy, love, unselfishness, service, purity, holiness, reached in the ripest experiences of earthly sainthood are only dim intimations of what we may become – ay, of what we shall become. Our life is hid, concealed, with Christ in God.

August 3

LIFE'S SENSITIVENESS

You go through a day of varying experiences, and everything that touches your life – the words you hear, the pictures you see, the books you read, the companions you meet and with whom you associate, the friendship that warms your heart – everything that touches you, leaves its mark on your character. And it is not a mere passing, transient impression that these things and these lives and experiences leave on your life; it is permanent work that they do. Not the great stones in the massive building are so wrought into the fabric as these impressions are wrought into the character. Our lives are temples, and every one who touches us is a builder. So it is also with the influences we throw off on other lives. They make their record there, and it is ineffaceable.

August 4

A CASKET OF SWEET THOUGHTS

When we learn to look up to God out of our weakness and sorrow, and say, 'Abba, Father,' what a revelation does the name disclose! what a treasure of precious love-thoughts does it unlock! For one thing, there is love in this divine Fatherhood – love that never falters, that never wearies, that stops at no sacrifice. There is also watchfulness that never sleeps, that looks down with compassionate eye from above the silent stars, and keeps vigil day and night. There is compassions, also, that peers into the depths of all our want and woe. There is shelter too, for ever does our Father stand between us and danger. There is guidance, a divine Hand clasping ours and leading us along through every strange way. No casket of earth's jewels holds so rich a cluster as does this heavenly casket, this name Father, contain of the jewels of divine grace.

August 5

THE MORAL POWER OF 'YES'

It is important that we learn to say 'Yes' when 'Yes' is the true answer. To all invitations upward to truer, deeper, richer, nobler life we should instantly answer 'Yes'. All calls to duty, to holy service, to noble deeds, to heroic battle, we should meet with glad 'Yes'. While we instantly shut our hearts against all that is impure and unholy, all thoughts that would tarnish or stain or blight, we should open them just as quickly to all thoughts that are pure and true and honest and just and lovely. One of the old Bible answers which we hear so often from the lips of saintly men, when called of God, is, 'Here am I.' It meant readiness for instant, unquestioning obedience. We need to get the same answer into our hearts vocabulary, that when God calls we may always respond with our prompt, ringing 'Here am I'

August 6

SPIRITUAL POVERTY

We are greedy after this world's things, and never can get enough of them; but of the real things, the things that will last through eternity, we are satisfied with very small portions. 'What seek ye?' asks the Master, his hands filled with precious blessings; and we ask for some little thing, some trifle, when we might have glorious fulness of blessing. How very strange it must seem to the angels to see us poor mortals giving our life, our very soul, to get some paltry things of earth that will perish tomorrow, and then not taking the precious spiritual boons that we might have for the mere asking!

August 7

UNSEEN BRETHREN

While we pour our kindness in perpetual benedictions upon those whose lives touch ours in our daily walks, we must not forget we have brethren whom we have never seen. Says the old proverb, 'There are people who live beyond the hill.' We must think of these in our planning for ourselves. We are in danger of living in a very small world, thinking of only a few people; but wherever there is a true follower of the Lord Jesus Christ, there is one of our brothers. He may be in India or China or Africa, or in some island of the sea; still he is our brother, and we ought to have some kindly thought for him.

August 8

GRIEF OFTTIMES AN EXCUSE

There are sorrows that hang no crape on the doorbell, and wear no black, and bow no shutters, and drop no tears that men can see, and can get no sympathy save that of Christ and perhaps a closest human brother. If you knew the inner life of many of the people you work with and do business with and meet socially in the common days, you would be very gentle with them; you would excuse their peculiarities, their absent-mindedness, their seeming thoughtlessness at times. Grief makes life hard for very many people. It is a wonder they can be as genial and loving as they are, in view of the burdens that crush them.

August 9

TESTING CHRIST'S WORDS

Every word of Christ comes to us with the challenge, 'Put me to the test. Try me. Prove me.' Religion is not a matter of theory, but a matter of life. We are to prove it by living it. Take every word which Christ speaks, and begin at once to obey it if it be a command, or trust it and lean on it if it be a promise. No matter if you do not understand it nor see why the command is good, yet do it. Let God lead you, and only be sure that you obey and trust him. You will not know any faster than you will do. Only keep on following Christ, and the way will open to you and become plain as you go on step by step.

August 10

CHRIST IN SUNSHINE

We are in danger of using our religion only in our dark hours, when we are in some trouble. But we need Christ just as much in our bright, prosperous, exalted hours as in the days of darkness, adversity and depression. His religion is just as much for our hours of joy as for our days of grief. There are just as many stars in the sky at noon as at midnight, although we cannot see them in the sun's glare. And there are just as many comforts and promises and divine encouragements and blessings above us when we are in our noons of human gladness and earthly success as when we are in pain and shadow.

August 11

ARE THERE LITTLE SINS?

We talk about little sins, but when we remember that every sin is committed against the infinite God, and that all sins are eternal in their influences and consequences, the smallest grows into stupendous importance. Indeed, there is nothing little in moral life. How do we know what is small or what is great in God's eye or as measured by its results through future ages? True faithfulness is not careless in little things. It is harder always to be faithful in small, obscure, unpraised things than in things that are brilliant and conspicuous. More persons fail in doing the little things, the common prosaic things, of everyday life than in doing the greater and more prominent things. Hence it is here that we need to keep double watch upon ourselves. All fraying out of character begins with one little thread left loose.

August 12

IMAGING CHRIST'S BEAUTY

Go and speak of Christ to others; tell them of his holiness, his purity, his mercy, his patience, his great love, his infinite gentleness; speak of his benign beauty till your face glows and your eyes shine with the lustre of his radiancy as you see it in his face. But do not fail to show them in your own character, in your disposition, in your love, patience, gentleness, sympathy, unselfishness, ministry, purity, some gleams, some radiant hints, of the beauty of Christ. Let people see in you at least a dim reflection of the beauty you praise.

August 13

FORGIVING INJURIES

Even those to whom we are the truest friends, and for whom we do the most, will sometimes treat us unjustly and do us sore injury. We cannot but feel the pain of such wrongs; but if meekly borne they will be turned to good for us by that divine love which transmutes everything into blessing for the life of faith. It is only when we cherish resentment and hold grudge in our hearts that the injuries done to us by others really harm us. Forgiveness robs them of their power to hurt us. Let us forgive generously. Too much of our forgiveness is with reservation: 'I forgive you; but this ends our friendship.' The fuller our forgiveness, the richer blessing do we take from the injurious treatment.

August 14

GOD'S GOODNESS IN ALL

It is not hard to believe in the divine goodness when all things are joyous. The hard thing is to believe in it just as firmly and quietly when all things seem against us. The goodness of God is just as surely and as richly revealed in the dark things of providence as in the bright things. God comes to us in many forms; but always his name is Love, always is he our Father. We keep two lists, and write some things as 'prosperous' and some as 'adverse'. God writes 'goodness' over all.

August 15

WHAT GRACE DOES NOT DO

Grace does not take trial out of human life. It does not make all the world feel kindly toward you. It does not hush the tongue of reproach and scorn. It does not quell the contentions of life. It does not soften human hardness nor destroy selfishness. It does not hush the sharp voices of criticism, fault-finding and frivolous talk. It does not command a truce to jealous rivalries and envyings, to personal abuse and silly strife. It does not say to the winds, 'Blow not on my child.' Christ makes no charmed circle about us where we shall never more feel the blast of the storm; but he gives a peace that will keep the heart calm and tranquil in the midst of the angriest strifes and storms.

August 16

WORKING BY FAITH

Faith links a man to Christ, so that he is no more a mere common man, with only his own poor feeble strength, but is more than a man – a man whom Christ is using, behind whom Christ's omnipotent energy is working. We must yield ourselves altogether to God and let him use us. Then his power, his wisdom, his skill, his thoughts, his love shall flow through our souls, our brains, our hearts, and our fingers. That is working by faith. It is simply putting our life into God's hand to be used, as one uses a pen to write or a brush to paint or a chisel to carve the statue.

August 17

RECEIVING CORRECTION PATIENTLY

Very many people are glad to correct others, and think it very strange they will not take the correction or criticism patiently, while if any one tries the same with them they quickly resent it. What is good for another sinner ought to be good for us too. Let us seek for grace to take correction from those who love us. If a friend tell us of a fault, let us not get angry, even if he does it awkwardly so as to give us pain. Let us thank him, and set about to cure the fault. Even from the lips of an enemy in anger we may yet get lessons it will do us good to learn.

August 18

BLESSING OF CONFLICT

We enter a world of antagonism and opposition the moment we resolve at Christ's feet to be Christians, to be true men and women, to obey God, to forsake sin, to do our duty. There never comes an hour when we can live nobly without effort, without making resistance to wrong influences, without struggle against the power of temptation. It never gets easy to be a worthy and faithful Christian. Sometimes we are almost ready to give it all up and to cease our struggling; but we should remember that the spiritual nobleness and beauty after which we are striving can become ours only through this very struggling.

August 19

BLESSINGS OF DARKNESS

We shall learn in the end, if only our faith fail not, that the best treasures of life and character come out of the dark painful hours. In days and nights of pain we learn endurance. In the struggles with doubt and fear we find at last bright blessed faith. In the darkness of sorrow we learn the song of joy. In weary suffering we get sweet pity for others. Meet every hard thing, every obstacle, every trial, every disappointment, every sorrow, with faith; be more than conqueror over it through Him that loved you, and it will leave blessing, treasure, enrichment, in your life.

August 20

CHRISTIAN CONVERSATION

There is a time for pleasantry and for humour. We are to talk about the bright, beautiful, joyful things around us. The Christian must not be sanctimonious. Religion suffers from nothing more than from cant. Our talk on business, on science, on pleasure, on whatever theme, should be fragrant with the perfumes of grace. An old proverb says: 'The heart and the tongue are only a span apart.' If a man's heart is touched by the fire of God, his lips will speak every words of beauty, truth, and gentle love on whatever theme he may speak.

August 21

OUR PERSONAL CREED

How many of us have taken our Bibles and put the doctrines of our creed to the proof? Our creeds might be shorter if we did this; yet if we only believed two or three great doctrines, and believed them after personal inquiry, and were able to tell why we believed them, it would be better than if we believed thirty-nine or forty or any number of doctrines merely because the Church teaches them. It is time we should begin to think earnestly about these things. Every Christian ought to be able to give an intelligent reason for the faith that is in him. Our personal creeds ought to grow out of our daily searching of the Word and our daily living.

August 22

NO STRANGE MYSTERY THERE

There are depths in the love of God vast and fathomless as the ocean, and we are only on the shore. Then there are strange things in God's providential dealings with each one of us. Death will solve a thousand mysteries for us in a moment. We will see then the reason for every trial, every pain, every loss, every disappointment. There will not be a trace of mystery left hanging about any providence. Love will glow everywhere. Then we shall see clearly, what now we know only by faith, that all things work together for good to them that love God.

August 23

LOVING UNLOVELY PEOPLE

There are some people whom it is very easy to love. They are congenial to our tastes. They have amiable qualities or charming manners, or they have befriended us, or they are our social companions. But there are others, good enough, yet not congenial, not amiable, not to our taste. They have unlovely and disagreeable traits. Faults mar the beauty of their character. Yet if we are Christians we should not fail to show brotherly love toward any. We must seek that charity that hides the multitude of sins and faults.

August 24

MISREPRESENTING CHRIST

If we are sour, peevish, easily provoked, surly, resentful, jealous, envious, bad-tempered in any way, what sort of impression of Christ do we give to those who know nothing of him save what they learn from our lives? Surely if we love Christ truly we will not allow ourselves to continue to do him dishonour by living a life so unworthy of his dear name. Whatever we may do for Christ, in gifts to his cause or work in his service, if we fail to live out his life of sweet patience and forbearance, we fail of an essential part of our duty as Christians.

August 25

THE WELL IN THE HEART

All noble life must be an inspiration from within, a well of water springing up, the spontaneous outflow of a full heart. We must seek to be filled with the divine Spirit. Then self will die. Then our life will breathe benedictions and drop blessings everywhere. Our very look will be full of kindness. We shall radiate light wherever we move, chasing away the darkness of others sorrow. Then, sharing our loaf with the hungry, our joy with the joyless, our strength with the fainting, Christ will give us more and more of comfort, joy, strength, and helpful power, and at last will share with us his own crown and glory. For the well in the heart springs up into everlasting life.

August 26

THE BLESSING OF TRUST

You cannot take into the innermost circle of your own heart's friends one who does not fully trust you. Doubt builds walls between hearts. Distrust hinders close fellowship. The same is true in friendship with Jesus. There must be perfect trust if we would get near to him. He knoweth them that trust in him. He feels the touch of every hand that rests in faith upon his arm. He feels the gentle pressure of every head that is laid upon his bosom. He hears every sweet breathing of confidence that goes up from our lips. Oh for that trust that, in every experience of sorrow and joy, remains calm and unbroken!

August 27

THE ONE PERFECT LIFE

Where do we find the truest, noblest life? There is no smallest fragment of our humanity that retains the absolute perfection and beauty that were in human life as it came first from the Creator's hand. If we would see life in its wholeness, unmarred, undebased – the highest, purest, truest life – we must look inside heaven. We are to become like Christ. We should never, therefore, lose sight of him. Keeping the ideal always before our eyes will, unconsciously yet powerfully, draw us toward itself.

August 28

NOT IN THE EASY PATHS

We are strongly tempted, in these luxurious days, to seek out the easy ways in life. Naturally we are not fond of bearing heavy burdens, of performing hard tasks, of making self-denials. We prefer to be indolent. Not many people die of overwork; more die of *ennui*. Souls are withered, too, by self-indulgence. It is a false idea that God has sown his blessings thickest amid the flowers of earth's gardens; nay, they lie thickest on the bare fields of hardship and toil. In shrinking from self-denials called for in the path of duty we are missing the best things God has to give us.

August 29

USELESSNESS OF WORRY

Worrying about your hard work does not make the work any easier, and it only makes you less strong and courageous for doing it. Worrying about some misfortune which you cannot help makes the misfortune no less and only renders its endurance harder. Thus far even common-sense goes. Then religion goes farther, and assures us that even the hard things, the obstacles and the hindrances, become blessings if we meet them in faith, stepping-stones upward, disciplinary experiences in which we may grow ever into nobler, stronger life.

August 30

TRUST BETTER THAN QUESTIONS

We ought not to ask questions about our Father's way – why he does this, why he does that. Surely it is better to trust our Father than to weary our brain with efforts to solve the mysteries and to find the reasons. Questions indicate fear or doubt; at least perfect trust asks no questions, does not seek to understand. It says, 'Even so, Father; for so it seemeth good in thy sight.' and rests there in perfect peace. Of course we cannot expect always to understand God's ways – he would not be God if we could; but we know that love is the key to them all, and that some time all shall be made clear even to us.

August 31

THE GREATEST WORK

We cultivate benevolence, charity, philanthropy, patriotism. We feed the hungry, and visit the sick, and minister to the poor, and provide for the widow and the orphan, and practise generosity. We emphasize personal character and service. We try to do good to men's bodies. We educate their minds. We seek their best interests in all physical and intellectual ways. All this is well so far as it goes; but we have not yet reached the greatests of all earthly things, the most important of all the work which a Christian can do. Are we striving to win souls? Are we seeking the lost to bring them to Christ? Saving souls is earth's greatest work.

SEPTEMBER

September 1

LIFE'S GREAT LESSONS

We all fail in the life-lessons which our great Teacher sets for us. The hardest school-tasks are easily mastered in comparison with the lessons of patience, sweet temper, forgiveness, unselfishness, humility, sweet temper, forgiveness, unselfishness, humility, purity, contentment. Even at best we can learn these lessons but slowly. And though but little seems to come from our yearnings and strugglings after Christ-likeness, yet God honours the yearning and the striving; and while we sit in the shadows of weariness, disheartened with our failures, he carries on the work within us, and with his own hands produces the divine beauty in our souls.

September 2

DEVOTION AND SERVICE

He who neglects love's duties of service, in Christ's name, cannot long enjoy the raptures of worship within the sanctuary. Devotion is not the end of Christian life; we wait upon God that we may renew our strength for noble service. In our eagerness to press within the temple to look upon the face of God, we must not pass unheeding by the suffering ones who lie with appealing glance and voice outside the temple-gate. Visions of God which lead to no active service will soon die out.

September 3

WHY ARE WE SO WEAK?

Every Christian ought to be an apostle of Christ, and ought to leave a shining record of blessed ministry all along his path. But how is it with many of us? Is there always power in our lives? Are we always victorious in temptation? Does life flow out from our lives in perpetual benedictions to others whom we touch or on whom our shadow rests? Is it not true of us that we continually fail to be, in the largest and best sense, blessings to others? Do we not come to Christ at the close of many of our days to lament our failure, and to ask him why we could not do the things we ought to do? Do we not all know what the answer is? – 'Because of your little faith.'

September 4

THE SIN OF THOUGHTLESSNESS

We try to excuse rude things or careless things we do that hurt others by saying, 'I didn't mean any unkindness.' Certainly we did not: it was not in our heart to be rude or brusque, or to give pain in any way. It was only 'want of thought'. Yes, but 'want of thought' is 'want of heart' – want of a gentle heart; for a gentle heart should always be thoughtful – love should never be thoughtless. We have no right to forget our relations to others and the duties of love we owe to them. Nothing can ever excuse a Christian for not being kindly, gentle, thoughtful, considerate.

September 5

GOD'S PLAN LIFE'S IDEAL

People sometimes sentimentalize over the constant changes and thwartings of plans and the disappointments of life. They grow morbid over them, and sigh, 'Vanity of vanities!' Or they ask, 'Why is the Lord dealing so sorely with me?' The success or non-success of our earthly plans is of very little consequence in comparison with the building up of Christ-likeness in our souls. Do not be surprised if you fail to have your own way at many a point. God would teach you that true success lies in the doing of his will, not your own, and the realizing of his plan for your life, not your plan.

September 6

WHAT WE OWE TO FRIENDSHIP

We do not know how much we owe to our true and pure friends – how much they add to our joy, what they do toward the formation and the adornment and enrichment of our character. We know not what touches, delicate and beautiful, on the canvas of our soul there will be for ever which the fingers of a friend have left there. There will be a silver thread in every life-web when finished, woven into the fabric by the pure friendship of many days. How important that only the true, the worthy, those with clean hands and good lives, be taken as friends! for an evil companionship will put stained and soiled threads into the web.

September 7

GOD'S LOVE CHANGELESS

Most of us have times when we can say, 'Oh, I know that God loves me now'; but the feeling is transient, and soon passes away. Tomorrow we are doubting and fearing as before, and the joy has gone out of our heart. Does God's love, then, change? Did he love me yesterday, and does he not love me today? Has the divine heart unclasped its hold upon me? No; the love of God is changeless and eternal. Heaven and earth may pass away, but the kindness of the Lord shall never depart from any of his children. Let us try to grasp this truth. Then, come what may, joy or sorrow, prosperity or adversity, we shall know always that the love of God abides unchanging – that we are held in its clasp with a hold that never can be torn loose.

September 8

BROTHERLY LOVE

There is no true love to Christ which does not also kindle in our hearts a corresponding love to men. He that loveth not his brother whom he hath seen cannot love God whom he hath not seen. Brotherly love is the very proof and badge of Christian discipleship. This love is not in name merely, but is real. It is a love that protects and helps; a love that keeps sacred watch over the good name of a brother, and by a strong arm averts the descending blow; a love that seeks every opportunity to bless and cheer and comfort; a love that serves and forgets self in loyal devotion even to death for a brother. In a word, it is 'as I have loved you'; and how does Christ love us? To answer this is to tell how he would have us love the brethren. We can thus read the meaning of the lesson in the blessed life of our Lord.

September 9

BESETTING SINS

The best things of life come to us wrapped up in difficulties, obstacles, seeming hindrances and oppositions, and unless we meet them heroically and victoriously we shall miss God's richest and best gifts and treasures. It is hard, for example, to have a besetting sin, one specially weak point, one temptation that comes perpetually up to us, stalking like a Goliath before us. Some of us know what it is to have sins which we do not overcome, which we do not even wrestle with, but which we allow to overcome us again and again. But do we not know that these very besetting sins are enemies that can be made friends to help us heavenward?

September 10

SILENT WORK

All the greatest work of this world goes on noiselessly. Only little workers clatter. God, both in nature and in grace, works silently. The angels go about noiselessly on their blessed ministries. So the best work any of us do is what we do without noise. Our words give forth sound, but it is not the sounds that do good, that brighten people's sad faces, that change tears to laughter, that stimulate hope, that put courage into fainting hearts; it is not the noise of our words, but the thoughts which the words carry. The best part of any good man's life is his influence – that strange, impalpable something which goes out evermore from his character like fragrance from a flower, like light from a star; and influence works always in silence, without words.

September 11

TAKING THOUGHT

There is one thing for which we are to take thought – not anxious, but very deep and earnest thought. We are to take thought about our duty, about our work, about doing God's will, and filling our place in God's world, and taking our part in advancing the heavenly kingdom. Too many people worry far more about their food and raiment, lest they shall be left to want, than they do about doing their whole duty. That is, they are more anxious about God's part in their lives than about their own part. They fear that God may not take care of them, but they do not seem to have any fear that they themselves may fail in duty or in fidelity to him.

September 12

THE BEAUTIFUL VISION

As the beauty of Christ's life and character glows before us in the light of the Gospels we should say, 'That is what I am to be some day. I am yet very far from it, but I am to reach it. That is my destiny.' Such a hope cherished in the heart has a wondrous uplifting power. Since we are to be some day like Christ, we should grow every day in grace; we should be getting ever a little more like Christ in feeling, in temper, in disposition, in affection; our aim should be to bring every thought and emotion and desire into sweet subjection to Christ. We should not only cherish the blessed vision, but should seek daily to grow into its divine beauty.

September 13

OUR FATHER'S HOUSE

We are in the Father's house in this world, though not in the best room of it, because sin has marred everything here. Still we are in the Father's house. His care is over us continually. His love pours its brightness all about us. His hand provides for our wants. Let us not think meanly of earth, for it is part of our Father's house. How near it brings heaven to us to think of it as but another room in the same house in which we were born and in which we have lived all our years! The life there is not a new life, but is simply the life we begin here continued there, with sin taken out and imperfection and all pain and suffering left for ever behind.

September 14

SAYING GOODBYES

Since any most hurried goodbye may be for years or may be for ever, should we not always part from our friends tenderly, kindly, lovingly? We should never separate in any angry mood, with bitterness in our hearts, with unforgiveness or misunderstanding we may never again have an opportunity to set right. We should never say goodbye carelessly or coldly, but with thoughtful love. We should strive to make our every briefest goodbye sweet and kindly enough for a last goodbye should it prove to be the last, as it may be.

September 15

RELIGION FOR ALL DAYS

Intense aspirations for holiness sometimes seem to unfit people for living in this world. Christ never meant it to be so, however, and such religion is wanting somewhere. You need a religion, not that will lift you up out of the weekday world into a seventh heaven of rapture, making you forget your duties to those about you, but a religion that will bring God down to walk with you in all the hard paths of toil and service, making even drudgery divine, and prosaic and commonplace toil a joy. That is what Christ wants to be to us.

September 16

GOD'S THOUGH FOR US

God has a plan for our life, for each individual life. There is something that he made us for; he has a thought in his mind for us, something he wants us to be and to do. Now we can never be what God wants us to be except by doing his will day by day. Disobedience or insubmission at any point will mar the perfectness of his plan for us. We know that whatever he wills for us is for us the highest possible good. God's will for us is always blessing. It will lead us at every step in the nearest way home. It will fashion in us each day a little more fully the image of Christ.

September 17

THE SAFEST PLACE

The safest place in all this world is ever the place of duty. God's wings are over it. God's peace guards it. It is said that at the centre of the cyclone there is a spot where there is almost perfect calm. A leaf there is scarcely stirred, and a baby would lie there unharmed. So at the centre of every great peril in life is a spot of holy calm where even the feeblest would not be harmed. It is the place of duty, of obedience, of the doing of God's will. He who stays there amid peril and trial is perfectly safe. No storm smites him, no plague comes nigh his dwelling. The way of duty is always a place of absolute safety. But he who departs from this charmed centre soon finds himself caught in the wild swirl and in peril. None of sin's ways are safe.

September 18

DYING GRACE

Many people worry because they do not seem to have 'dying grace'. They still fear death and shrink from it. But God has never promised dying grace when one's duty is to *live*. Grace for duty, for toil, for love, for honesty, for earnest service in every good cause, for brave struggle, for unselfish ministry, for holy influence; grace for noble and beautiful living, and for loyal devotion to Christ while the heart's pulses are full and while God wants us still in this world – but not yet grace for dying since death is far away. Then grace for dying when the life's work is done, its duty finished, and the call comes to leave this world and go home. And will not that be soon enough for dying grace to be bestowed?

September 19

THE TOUCH OF CHRIST

No one can read the gospel story without being impressed with the marvellous power of Christ's touch. Wherever it was felt blessing came. We find ourselves sometimes mourning the loss of this touch, and wishing that we could feel it and get its benediction. But really we have not lost it. Christ has indeed passed out of our sight into the heavens, but his hand is stretched out still. It is laid just as of old upon sufferers, and has lost none of its power to comfort, to heal, to open blind eyes. Christ lays his hand upon our heads every time we bow at his feet in prayer. When we are in trouble he comes and comforts us with his warm touch of sympathy. When we are sick or in pain he is by our bed, and his hand is laid on our fevered brow to give rest and peace.

September 20

SERVING CHRIST FOR HIMSELF

We are ready for usefulness just in the measure in which we have learned the lesson of self-forgetfulness. Self stands in the way of many glorious possibilities of good. Men drag their own personality into the cause they are serving. They stickle for honour and place, and demand recognition, appreciation and reward. Appreciation and gratitude are very sweet. Who does not love to receive words of commendation? But if such words do not come – if, instead, wrong and injustice come – our zeal for Christ should be no less intense. Let us so sink ourselves in the cause of Christ that our loyalty, devotion, and fidelity shall in no way be affected either by honour or neglect, by praise or blame.

September 21

TO MAKE MEN BETTER

Our mission as Christians in this world is to do good to the worst people, to comfort, to help, to bless, to save. We are debtors to all men. We owe to every one we meet some benediction. We have an errand to every one. Where we can see no beauty, we are to seek to put the beauty of holiness; where we find only enmity and rage and wrong, we are to seek by patient love to overcome the evil with good. So, always forgetting ourselves and our rights, we are to strive to save others for heaven. If we go among men with this motive in our hearts, we shall have great joy in doing good even to the lowliest.

September 22

PEACE BEFORE MINISTRY

We are in no condition for good work of any kind when we are fretted and anxious in our minds. It is only when the peace of God is in our heart that we are ready for true and helpful ministry. A feverish heart makes a worried face, and a worried face casts shadows wherever the person goes. A troubled spirit mars the temper and the disposition. It makes the whole life less beautiful. It unfits one for giving cheer and inspiration, for touching other lives with good and helpful impulses. Peace must come before ministry. It was when Jesus had touched the sufferer's hand and the fever had left her that she arose and ministered unto her friends.

September 23

BEYOND PAIN'S VALLEY

Many of the richest possibilities of prayer lie beyond valleys of pain and sorrow. The best things of life cannot be gotten save at sore cost. When we pray for more holiness we do not know what we are asking for; at least we do not know the price we must pay to get that which we ask. Our 'Nearer, my God, to thee,' must be conditioned by, and often can come only through, 'e'en though it be a cross that raiseth me.' Not only are the spiritual things the best things, but many times the spiritual things can be grasped only by letting go and losing out of our hands the earthly things we would love to keep. God loves us too much to answer prayers for comfort and relief, even when we make them, if he can do it only at spiritual loss to us. He would rather let it be hard for us to live, if there is blessing in the hardness, than make it easy for us at the cost of the blessing.

September 24

GOD'S DARK ROOM

The noblest, richest, purest and most fruitful lives in this world have always been lives of sufferers. There are elements of loveliness in the depths of every human soul which the fires of pain alone can bring out. The photographer carries his picture into a darkened room to develop it. God often takes his children into the chamber of pain and draws the curtains while he brings out the features of his own image, which before had been there in but dim and shadowy outlines.

September 25

THE HUMAN NOT ENOUGH

Sometimes we are in danger of putting our trust in our human friends rather than in the divine Friend. God comes to us still in human forms. He reveals his sympathy and love through human hearts. He speaks to us through human lips. He guides us by human hands. But if the human be all we get, if we do not learn to cling to God, and lean upon the divine arm beneath the human arm, and look to God for the blessings we want, dark for us will be the hour when the human falls away and we are left alone in the darkness. Wherever, in whatever form and whomsoever you are led first to know God, be sure that it is God you know and trust.

September 26

MISINTERPRETATION

Life is full of misinterpretations. Many of us have wrong opinions of others. We think they do not care for us when they really do. We imagine they are angry at us when there is not a shade of unkind feeling in their heart. We misinterpret their acts. Many a time things that offend us, if we but understood the motive that prompted them and the true love that is in them, would appear really beautiful in our eyes. We ought to guard continually against these misinterpretations. They do wrong to others. They rob our own hearts of peace. 'Love thinketh no evil.' Let us be sure always that we see an act in its proper light.

September 27

LITTLE WHITE LIES

People talk about 'white lies' – little deceptions, concealments, false seemings, subterfuges – as if they were not particularly wrong. But he who would be true must be true through and through, in the innermost depths of his being and in the smallest affairs as well as the largest. He must simply be true. Let your soul of truth be as pure and unstained as the snowflakes when they fall from the cloud. There really are no 'white lies'; all lies are black. Falsehood is of the night, no matter whether it be merely a look or a silence that deceives, or whether it be an uttered untruth. Let us learn to be true for God's eye.

September 28

SUCH AS WE HAVE

We can do a great deal of the wisest, truest good among men without giving money. A strong hand reached out to help a fallen one rise again is better than money. New hope and fresh courage put into a discouraged heart are better than money. True comfort, enabling one in sorrow to pass through it sustained and victorious, is better than money. Let no one say he cannot do anything for others unless he has money to give. Use what you have. Heart-coins, life-coins, are better than coins from the mint. The things we do for men's souls are far more to them than the things we do merely for their bodies. Besides, all God asks us to give to others is of such as we have.

September 29

GOD GUIDING OUR STEPS

'Order my steps' is a prayer which should ever be on our lips. We should get our orders from God, not once in our life only, when we first give ourselves to him; not at the opening of each day only, as we go forth to the day's task – but every moment, for each step. That is what walking with God means. We may make this so real that we shall look up into God's face continually, asking, 'What next, dear Lord? What shall I do now? Which course shall I take today? How shall I do this duty?' If we can but have God's guidance and help for the little short steps, we need not fear for the long miles, the great stretches of road. If each step is of his ordering, the long miles will be paths of his choosing.

September 30

EMPTY HANDS

Full hands at the end of a life do not always tell of true success. Earthly failure is ofttimes higher success in God's eyes than what men regard as success. Scars of wounds gotten in conflict and strife with sin are more splendid marks of honour, when the hands are held up before God, than diamonds and gold and crowns gained by yielding in life's conflicts. Strive to get your hands filled with the invisible things of God's heavenly kingdom. Fight the battles of life heroically, and never mind the scars. Better have wounded and empty hands that are clean than hands that are full and yet are stained with sin.

OCTOBER

October 1

MIXING WORK WITH BRAINS

It is a good thing to think. The more thought we put into our work the better it will be done. Work of all kinds becomes exalted, ennobled, refined and produces good, lasting effects just in proportion as men put thought into it. All worthy, noble, useful, beautiful living must have its dark quarries of purposing, thinking, planning, shaping, polishing, behind its being and doing. Look well to the quarries, and you need not give much thought to the rising of the building. Prepare no stained blocks in your heart-quarries. Train yourself to think only pure thoughts – white, clean thoughts.

October 2

MAKING PERFECT WORK

'Trifles make perfection,' replied the artist to one who asked him why he spent so much time in giving the little finishing-touches to his statue. There can be no perfection in any kind of workmanship unless attention be paid to the minutest details, the merest trifles of construction or finishing. One smallest flaw or incompleteness left in the work, in any part of it, leaves a blemish on the finished endeavour. Life is a mosaic, and each smallest stone must be polished and set with greatest care or the piece will not at last be perfect. One whose daily life is careless is always weak in character. But one who habitually walks in right paths, no matter how small and apparently trifling the things may be, grows strong and noble. Trifles make perfection.

October 3

GROWING THROUGH STRUGGLE

The nominal Christian life that costs nothing is not worthy of the name. There must be self-restraint, discipline, severe schooling. There must be struggle, the agonizing effort. If you are to reach the goal and win the prize, you must put every energy of your life into the race. There must be sacrifice of indolence and self-will and personal ease. Too much pampering spoils many an earnest Christian. Every noble life is a struggle from beginning to end. Only those who resist and fight and overcome are successful in life. This is true in every sphere – in business, in study, in professional life and in spiritual life. Are we resisting sin, overcoming temptation, living victoriously in trial? If not, we are not living worthily.

October 4

APPRECIATION TOO LATE

We ought not to need night to teach us the glories of the day. We ought not to have to wait for sorrow before we can appreciate the sweetness of joy. Yet is it not often true that we learn the value of our blessings by their loss? Many a time an empty chair is the first full revealer of the worth and faithfulness of a precious human friendship. Would it not be well if we were to seek to appreciate our good things while we have them? We would then have the joy itself, and not merely the dull pain of regret as we look back at blessings vanished. Besides, we would do more for our friends while they are with us if we appreciate their worth. Too many of us never understand what we owe to our dear ones until their remains no further opportunity of paying love's debt.

October 5

THE DIVINE GUIDANCE

No ancient pillar ever made the way more plain to those who watched it for guidance than does God's providence make the path of duty in common days for those who truly acknowledge God and desire his guidance. It is not because we cannot know God's way that we do not see it, but because we want instead to take our own way. There is no use in our looking into our Lord's face and asking, 'What now, dear Master?' if we do not mean to take the path he marks out. We must have the spirit of obedience if we are to receive the divine direction. 'Not my will, but thine,' must be the prayer of our heart, cost what it may to surrender our own and take God's.

October 6

THE DIVINENESS OF SERVICE

You believe that the life of Jesus Christ was the noblest life ever lived in this world. No king of earth ever attained such splendid, such real royalty as did he. No human hero on battlefield ever did deeds of such inherent greatness as those wrought by the hands of the Carpenter of Nazareth. And what was the ruling spirit of his life? Was it not service? 'Not to be ministered unto, but to minister,' was the motto of all his beautiful years. He lived wholly for others. He never had one thought for himself, never did the smallest act for himself. At last he emptied out his very blood in the greatest of all his acts of service. Shall we not learn from our Lord's example that the truest life in this world is one of self-forgetting love? Selfishness anywhere mars and spoils the beauty of the rarest deed. We must get the spirit of service, and then our lives shall be Christ-like.

October 7

GETTING SORROW'S BLESSING

To all, in some form or other, suffering will sometime come; but if it is borne in the true way it will bring rich blessings. It will produce in us, even in this world, the fruits of righteousness. It will make us greater blessings to others, since the things we learn in pain we can teach in joy and song. Are you in sorrow? Do not fail to get the blessing from it that it has certainly brought to you from God. It is only when we do the right thing in our troubles that they do us good. Many people let their cares and worries into their hearts, and when they do this their lives are spoiled and harmed, and not blessed, by them. It is only when we keep God's peace within us in sorrow that we get the benediction.

October 8

OTHER PEOPLE'S CONVENIENCE

We ought to think of other people's convenience more than some of us do. The home is the place where this thoughtfulness ought to begin and be cultivated. One who comes late to breakfast admits that he is guilty of an amiable self-indulgence but forgets that he has marred the harmonious flow of the household life, and caused confusion and extra work. The other day an important committee of fifteen was kept waiting for ten minutes for one tardy member, who came sauntering in at last without even an apology for having caused fourteen men a loss of time that to them was very valuable, besides having put a sore strain on their patience and good nature. Common life is full of just such thoughtlessnesses, which cause untold personal inconvenience, and ofttimes produce irritation and hurt the hearts of friends. We ought to train ourselves in all our life to think also of other people.

October 9

RELIGION IN THE COMMON DAYS

One of the most harmful practical errors of common Christian living is the cutting of life into two sections – a religious and a secular section. We acknowledge God in the religious part. We fence off days and little spaces of time in each day which we profess to give to worship, devotion. But the danger is that we confine our acknowledging of God to these set times and seasons, while we shut him out of our real life. That is not true religion which prays well, and soars away into celestial raptures and holy dreams, while it has no effect on one's daily common life down here in the paths of toil and duty. We should have our visions, but we must bring them down into our earthly experience and make them real there.

October 10

SERVING CHRIST IN HIS PEOPLE

When we lay our lives at Christ's feet in consecration, and tell him that we want to serve him with them, he gives them back to us again, and bids us use them in serving his people, our fellow-men. In the humblest and the lowliest of those who bear Christ's image Christ himself comes to us. We do not know when he stands before us in a lowly one who needs our sympathy or our help. It would be a sad thing if we turned him away unfed from our doors some day, or neglected to visit him in his sickness. Let us not say we love Christ, if we are not ready to serve those whom he sends to us to be served.

October 11

SOLITARINESS OF LIFE

We talk about companionship in life, and they certainly are very sweet. There is immeasurable helpfulness in strong, true friendships. Still, it is true that however many, faithful, and sympathetic our friends may be, we must enter and pass through all life's crises alone. Every one of us lives really a solitary life. We do not fight in companies and battalions and regiments, but as individuals. Each one must live his own life. 'Every one must bear his own burden.'

'Why should we faint and fear to live alone,
   since all alone (so Heaven has willed) we die?
Not even the tenderest heart, and next our own,
   Knows half the reasons why we smile and sigh.'

October 12

THE EFFECTS OF WORDS

There are words spoken quietly and coldly which break like the lightning-flash, bearing on their blighting wings sad desolation which years cannot repair. On the other hand, there are simple words which, treasured in memory, hang like bright stars of joy and cheer in dark nights of sorrow and trial. Keep ever speaking true words, kindly, loving words, the words of Christ, wherever you go, and you will some day find them again in benedictions in the hearts of those who have heard them.

October 13

THE PATH OF GLORY

The path of glory for a life lies not far away among the cold mountains of earthly honour, nor yet in any paths of fame where worldly ambition climbs, but close beside us, in the lowly ways of Christ-like ministry. He who stoops to serve the poor and the suffering, in Christ's name, will find at length that he has served Christ himself. Jesus lives in this world in his people, in every one of them, in the least of them – the poorest, the obscurest, the most down-trodden and despised. He calls them all 'my brethren'. The smallest kindness done to one of them he accepts as though done to himself in person.

October 14

PROMISES IN RESERVE

He who has not in the sunny days made the divine promises his own has no comforts to sustain him when trouble comes. But he who has pondered the Scriptures, and laid up in memory the precious truths and assurances, when called to pass through affliction has light in his dwelling. Words of promise in which he had never before seen any special comfort shine out now like stars when the sun has gone down; or, like lamps above his head, unnoted before, they pour their soft beams upon his soul. This is a provision all of us should make in youth and health and happiness for the dark days that will surely come.

October 15

LIFE A STEWARDSHIP

We are not all apostles in the same sense that St. Paul was; but to every one of us Christians Christ has given a solemn and sacred trust in our own salvation. We are to be true to him in a world of sin and temptation. We are to be faithful to duty wherever we stand. We each have a mission which we must strive to fulfil. Are we keeping the faith, true to every sacred trust which God has placed in our hands? Are we taking care of the part of the vineyard assigned to us, and rendering of the fruits to him who has committed it to our care? Not to fulfil our mission is soon to be left without a mission, dropped out, set aside, while others do our work and receive the honour and reward which would have been ours.

October 16

WHAT GOD CROWNS

The 'crown of righteousness' is not given for much service or for great sacrifices, but for Christ-like character. The crown is in reality the efflorescence of the life itself, its bursting into glory and beauty, and is not something else, however brilliant, prepared and brought and set upon the head. The *crown* of righteousness is righteousness in character, blossoming into heavenly radiance under the smile of God. Let us not forget that tireless activity is not enough to win this crown; that heroic struggle is not enough. We must be holy, sanctified in our moral nature, righteous in life and character. It is not what we do that is crowned, but what we are.

October 17

THE WISDOM THAT WINS

It is not worldly wisdom that is required to win souls – great learning, knowledge of science and philosophy. It is spiritual wisdom that is needed – the wisdom that comes down from God, the wisdom of faith, of love, of prayer, of humility. It is the wisdom Christ gave his disciples before he sent them out. Soul-winning is earth's holiest work. He who adds the least touch of beauty to a sacred life does more than he who paints a masterpiece; but he who brings a lost soul to the Saviour, who seeks and finds a wandering sheep and bears it back to the fold, does the noblest, greatest work possible on this earth.

October 18

A LAMP FOR THE FOOTPATH

God's Word as a guiding light is a *lamp* unto our *feet*, not a sun flooding a hemisphere. It is not meant to shine upon miles of road, but in the darkest night it will always show us the one next step; then when we have taken that, carrying the lamp forward, it will show us another step, and thus on till it brings us out into the full, clear sunlight of coming day. It is a lamp, and it is designed to lighten only little steps, one by one. We need to learn well the lesson of patience if we would have God guide us. He does not lead us rapidly. Sometimes we must go very slowly if we wait for him. Only pace by pace does he take us and unless we wait, we must go in darkness. But if we wait for him, it will always be light for one step.

October 19

THE SIN AND PERIL OF FAILURE

To be faithless in duty is to lose all the blessing which is promised to those who are loyal and true. No matter how perilous the duty that comes to you, you cannot decline it save at your own peril. The only safe way in life's thronging field is straight on in the path of duty. No duty, however perilous or hard, should be feared half so much as *failure* in the duty. Stand where Christ places you, and be simply true – that is all. Make no effort to be great. The greatest thing possible to you any day is faithfulness. Only be faithful. He requires no more of the highest angel in glory.

October 20

IMMORTALITY OF ACTIONS

Since every impression is enduring; since every act leaves its mark on the life itself, as well as on other lives; since the smallest things we do become parts of our own being, while they also touch and affect others – what tremendous destinies are folded up in each quiet day of ours! The things you are doing these swift hours are for eternity. The words you spoke yesterday for Christ in the ear of the weary sufferer, the strong, helpful words you spoke to the discouraged one, the tempted one, the burdened one, the thought of comfort you breathed softly and with a prayer in the home of grief – do you know that the ministry of these good words will never cease?

October 21

AFTER-VIEWS THE TRUEST VIEWS

The real character of actions is seen only when we look at them from the side next eternity. You had a duty to perform which at the time was a cross to you. It required courage. It involved self-denial and personal sacrifice. It was very hard to do. You look back upon it, however, and it appears a beautiful act, and you are not sorry you made the sacrifice. This after-view is the true one. Sin in the form of temptation seems fascinating, but sin committed looks horrible. Again the after-view is the true one. The point from which we see a human life in its truest light is its end, looking back over it from the edge of eternity. The false colours fade out in the light of the judgment.

October 22

LIVING OUT GOD'S THOUGHTS

Let your highest ambition be to become what God has planned for you. Lay all your plans at his feet. Let God's will be your will, and he will lead you to just that life which will be for you the most beautiful, the most honourable, and the most blessed. If you would have God's thoughts to live out in your life, you must go to God for them. You must sit down often with him in the silence. You must look reverently into the divine Word and ponder deeply its holy sentences. You must turn your steps habitually to the place of prayer. You will not have heavenly visions if you never look upward for them.

October 23

CLIMBING BY SELF-CONQUEST

Every low desire, every bad habit, all longings for ignoble things, ll wrong feelings that we conquer and trample down, become ladder-rounds for our feet, on which we climb upward out of grovelling and sinfulness into nobler, grander life. If we are not living victoriously these little common days, we are not making any progress in true living. Only those who climb are getting toward the stars. Heaven at last, and the heavenly life here, are for those who overcome.

October 24

SILENCE UNDER CALUMNY

Any of us may sometime become the innocent victim of calumny. Pure in our heart and life, we may have to endure suspicion of evil. As Christians, what should we do? In some cases vindication may be possible, and it may be our duty to seek it in the right way. But there may be instances when we cannot free ourselves without bringing dishonour upon others. Then we must be silent and bear our load. We are not likely to err in the direction of too great patience and silence under wrong; our danger lies the other way. So let us beware lest, when others injure us or defame us, we sin against God in trying to vindicate ourselves. Let us rather suffer, and leave our vindication with God – committing ourselves to him who judgeth righteously.

October 25

NOT CLAIMING OUR PRIVILEGES

Are not many of us conscious that we are living far below our privileges? Do we not understand that we are not as good Christians, as rich in character, as fruitful in life, as we might be? Do we not know that there is a possible fulness of spiritual blessedness which we have not yet attained? Why is it? Is there any want in God, from whom all good gifts come? Is not the reason in ourselves? Is it not because we cling to other things, earthly things, which fill our hearts and leave but small room for Christ? We have not the hunger for righteousness, for holiness, and though there is abundance of provision close before us, yet our souls are starving. If we would have the abundant life which Christ wants to give us, we must empty out of our hearts the perishing trifles that fill them, and make room for the Holy Spirit. We must pray for spiritual hunger; for only to those who hunger comes the promise of filling and satisfying.

October 26

LOVE – MINISTRY

Love for Christ in human hearts shapes itself into manifold forms of gentle, helpful ministry, according to the quality, the circumstances, and the relations of each life. What we need to make sure of is that we truly have the spirit of service, 'the mind that was in Christ Jesus.' It is not great deeds that God expects or requires of us, unless he has endowed us with large gifts and has given us great things to do. He gives us certain talents and puts us in certain relations, and then asks us to be faithful – nothing more. The man with the plain gifts and the small opportunities is not expected to do the great things that are required of the man with the brilliant talents and the large opportunities. 'She hath done what she could' is the highest approving word that could be spoken of any one, and it may be only for a smile of love and a crust given in Christ's name.

October 27

THE BLESSEDNESS OF DEATH

Christian life in this world is not a voyage in the sunshine, darkening as it progresses and growing stormy, ending in utter wreck on death's shores; rather, it is a voyage through earthly storm and shadow, but at last out into the broad ocean of eternal blessedness. Death is not the end, but the beginning. It is not loss, but gain. It is not into darkness, but into marvellous light. It is not to silence and stillness, but into life far more real and active. It is not away from joy and gladness and beauty, but is out of the mere hints and shadows and hopes of blessedness into the full revelation of Christ, into his very presence, where there is fulness of joy, where there are pleasures for evermore.

October 28

FINISHING OUR WORK

God first puts the good thoughts and the holy impulses into your heart. Then when you try to obey and do what he commands and suggests, he helps you to do it. 'It is God which worketh in you both to will and to work.' If character is a web and we are weavers, we cannot ourselves prepare white, clean threads of thought and purpose and love, for our hearts are unclean; nor can we weave the threads into a pure, unsoiled web, for our hands are stained. God must put into our hearts the beautiful threads. He must give us the pattern, too, into which he would have us fashion the fabric. Then he must cleanse our hands and guide our fingers. In weaving this web we must not miss a thread, for if we do the loom goes on and the web rolls by, but the place of the dropped thread remains unfilled. Would you be able to say at your life's end, 'I have finished the work which God gave me to do,' you must be sure that each smallest duty is done in its own time. To have at last a finished life, each day must close with its duty all done, no tasks remaining unfinished. That is, each day's work must be left complete, with life's duty done up to that moment, as if we should never come again to our tasks.

October 29

SERVING THE HIGHEST LIFE

God gives us in the darkness of this world many glimpses of heaven's blessed life. The Scriptures are full of windows through which the light pours. And every disclosure of heavenly existence that is made to us shows us life without one trace of selfishness, earnestly devoted to the service of others. Angel-life is very pure, holy, and blessed, and yet these celestial beings, the angels, find their employment in serving. It is their joy to minister, not to be ministered unto. If we would be as angels, we must have to same spirit. Then the Son of God came, and his life's spirit was described in his own words, 'the Son of man came not to be ministered unto, but to minister.' Serving is therefore the most exalted, the divinest thought of life.

October 30

OBEDIENCE TO IMPULSES

We all have our impulses to duty. We know what we ought to do. What do we do with the calls of duty and the cries and appeals of human distress? Do we allow them to die away unheeded? If we do, our own souls shall be losers. We walk about at home, and we see heathenism, misery, and squalor under the very shadows of our churches. We catch on all hands the sobs and moanings of human distress. And we are ordained by Christ to carry his salvation, his comfort, his grace to our fellow-men. The news of God's love which has come to you is not for yourself; you get the full, rich blessing of it only when you tell it to some other. Do we obey these divine impulses?

October 31

TRAINING THE TEMPER

Temper itself is not an evil power, a demoniacal possession, in any one. Temper may make irreparable mischief if allowed to run untamed, but when brought under the sway of a sanctified will it becomes an element of great power. A strong temper held in perfect leash gives majesty to the life. And there is no temper which cannot be brought under control through God's help. Let none of us despair, therefore, if we have a strong temper which ofttimes leads us to sinful outbursts. We can tame our temper until the most impatient of us shall become and shall remain calm and quiet under the sorest provocation. Yet we shall never get past the need of watchfulness, for a conquered lion is a lion still if the old spirit is aroused.

NOVEMBER

November 1

GOD NEEDS OUR FAITHFULNESS

God's providence is always good, but he needs our faithfulness, our truest and best work always, to give full expression and result to the good that he plans. It is possible for us to mar the good that God intends, and to turn his work into disaster that he never intended. God never does his work unfaithfully, and we dare not charge to his providence the preventable accidents of life, those which come through men's carelessness or dishonesty or greed of gain or fault of any sort. We must remember that even the providence of God cannot work completely or perfectly without our little work, each and every one's little work, well done.

November 2

THE RADIANT IDEAL

We may become like angels. What debasement, then, to let our lives, with all their glorious possibilities, be dragged down into the dust of shame and dishonour! Rather let us seek continually the glory for which we were made and redeemed. 'Beloved, now are we children of God, and it is not yet made manifest what we shall be. We know that, if he shall be manifested, we shall be like him; for we shall see him even as he is. And every one that hath this hope set on him purifieth himself, even as he is pure.'

'Wonderful the whiteness of thy glory!
Can we truly that perfection share?

Yes; our lives are pages of thy story,
    We thy shape and superscription bear.
Tarnished forms – torn leaves – but thou canst mend them;
    Thou thine own completeness canst unfold
From our imperfections, and wilt end them –
    Dross consuming, turning dust to gold.'

November 3

AMUSEMENT AS A MEANS OF GRACE

Amusement must never become an end in life; it must always be a means, a help on the way, just as sleep is, just as rest is. An hour's amusement should be to you just what a night's sleeping is, or what a day's resting is: it should make you stronger, clearer-headed, calmer-souled, braver, more hopeful, more earnest, more enthusiastic, inspiring you for better life. Anything that leaves a taint of impurity upon the life or starts a thought of impurity in the mind, anything that degrades or debases the soul, is unfit and unworthy amusement for a Christian. Christian amusements must be such as do not harm spiritual life; they must be means of grace.

November 4

SILENCES THAT ARE SINFUL

In every life there are times when to be silent is to fail in duty. We are to speak out on all occasions when the glory of Christ demands it. We should never fear to speak the word of warning to one in danger. We should never hesitate to speak boldly in confession of Christ in the presence of his enemies. To be ashamed of him is a grievous wrong to him. Many of us sin, too, by our silence toward hearts that are hungry for love. On our tongues lie the words that would give blessing, but we hold our peace and let the sad hearts break. Many of us talk too much, no doubt – 'speech is silver and silence is golden' – but let us remember also that 'there is a time to speak'.

November 5

COST OF HELPING OTHERS

It is only when you have passed through the fierceness of temptation, wrestling with evil, sore beset, and victorious only through the grace of Christ, that you are ready to be a helper of others in their temptation. It is only when you have known sorrow in some form yourself, and when you have been comforted by divine grace and helped to endure, that you are fitted to be a comforter of others in their sorrow. You must learn before you can teach, and the learning costs. At no small price can we become true helpers of others in this world. Lessons which cost us nothing are worth but little. Virtue went out of Jesus to heal others; virtue must go out of us to become life and benediction to other souls.

November 6

THE HEART OF PRAYER

Mere words do not make prayer. The repeating of forms of petition, however beautiful they may be or however eloquently uttered, is not praying. There must be fire – the fire of love glowing upon the golden altar of the heart. There must be sincere worship of soul, there must be fervency of spirit, there must be warm, earnest desire. The prayer must be kindled in the heart by the love of God shed abroad by the Holy Spirit. Unless our very heart goes into our forms of words, borne on faith's wings and pressing to God's feet, we do not really pray.

November 7

THE TRANSFORMING LOOK

Keeping the eye upon the likeness of Christ transfigures the life. The old monks intently gazed upon the crucifix, and they said that the print of the nails would come in their hands and feet, and the thorn-scars in their brow, as they beheld. It was but a gross fancy, yet in the fancy there is a spiritual truth. Gazing by faith upon Christ, the lines of his beauty indeed print themselves on our hearts. That is the meaning of St. Paul's words – 'We all, with unveiled face, beholding as in a mirror the glory of the Lord, are transformed into the same image.' The gospel is the mirror. There we see the image of Christ. If we earnestly, continuously, and lovingly behold it, the effect will be the changing of our own lives into the same likeness. The transformation is wrought by the divine Spirit, and our part is only to behold, to continue beholding, the blessed beauty. We sit before the camera, and our own picture is printed on the prepared glass. We sit before Christ, and we become the camera, and his image is printed on our soul.

November 8

EMPTY CONVERSATION

Christian conversation should not be a mere jargon of empty, idle words. There are many people who talk incessantly and never say anything worth repeating or remembering. They never give any comfort to those who are in trouble. They never incite those who hear them to anything noble or good. Their words if gathered up would be millions of blossoms, and not one handful of fruit; tons of sand, and not one shining sparkle of gold. Surely such conversation is not worthy of immortal beings, children of God and heirs of glory, on their way home to glory.

November 9

LET THE BLESSING FLOW OUT

While you are to brighten first the place nearest to you, you are also to throw the little beams of your lamp as far as they will reach. It will not make your home any less bright if, on a dark night, you open the shutters of your windows and let some of the brilliancy and the cheer pour out upon the street. Then others, too, may be blessed by the light that fills your home. If you have a beautiful garden, why should you build a high wall around it to hide it from the eyes of passers-by? Would it not be a more Christ-like thing to tear down your stone wall and let all that move along the street be blessed and cheered by the beauty?

November 10

ON LOOKING FOR SLIGHTS

We must look to ourselves and take heed how we receive the acts, the words, and the manners of others. If we are proud, and are always on the watch for slights and unfriendly hints and little hurts, we can find plenty of them. We need, therefore, to cultivate the spirit of humility in all our intercourse with others. We need to learn patience, forbearance, longsuffering, meekness, forgiveness; in a word, love – love that thinketh no evil. Then we shall never be suspicious, never be exacting, never demand our 'rights'. We shall endure even intended wrongs patiently, sweetly, with true meekness.

November 11

THE WINSOMENESS OF LOVE

'God loves you and I love you,' says Mr. M'All to the poor people he would lift up. There is little use in telling people the first part of this message if we cannot tell them also the second part, or at least make them see it in our face, in our words and acts, in our true, tireless interest in them. The love of Christ must throb in our own hearts, and shine in our eyes, and speak in our words, and offer itself again on the cross in our lives, in our efforts to save others, if we would win souls for heaven. We must love the people we would win. We must have some conception of the infinite value of the lives we try to save in order that we may love them. Without this we cannot deeply and truly care for those whom sin has stripped of beauty. But if we understand their real worth and the possibilities there are in their lives, it will not be hard for us to love even the farthest away from God.

November 12

KEEP THE IDEAL UNDIMMED

We each have in our soul, if we are true believers in Christ, a vision of spiritual loveliness into which we are striving to fashion our lives. This vision is our conception of the character of Christ. 'That is what I am going to be some day,' we say. Far away beyond our present attainment as this vision may shine, yet we are ever striving to reach it. This is the ideal which we carry in our heart amid all our toiling and struggling. This ideal we must keep free from all marring or stain. We must save it though we lose our very life in guarding it.. We should be willing to die rather than give it up to be destroyed. We should preserve the image of Christ, bright, radiant, unsoiled, in our soul until it transforms our dull, sinful, earthly life into its own transfigured beauty.

November 13

DO NOT WORRY

We have nothing to do with tomorrow until we get to it. When the day comes with its cares, then we may meet them and then God will provide for them. Duty only is ours – the faithful, diligent doing of God's will day by day. The rest is God's, and anxious care is unbelief. Our Father will surely take care of us if we are only faithful to him. Away, then, with anxiety. Do your work, your duty, the bit of God's will for the day, and let God care for you. Then the peace of God shall keep your heart and mind.

November 14

PROMOTION BY FAITHFULNESS

We are always on trial in this world. God's promotions are all in the line of fidelity. When we do well with one talent, he puts two in to our hand. When we show ourselves faithful and capable with two, he adds two more. This is true not only of ordinary business capacities and fidelities, but also of moral and spiritual powers and privileges. When we do anything well, God increases our responsibilities, puts new trusts into our charge. But failure in any testing brings the loss of the trusts already in our hands. If we would grow into great usefulness, we must be ever watchful that we fail in no duty or trial.

November 15

LOOKING FOR BLESSINGS

Do we take the blessings that the common days bring to us? Do we extract the honey from every flower that grows by our path? Do not angels come to us unawares in homely or unattractive disguise, walk with us, talk with us, and then only become known to us when they have flown away – when their places are empty? Shall we not learn to see the goodness and the beauty in the gifts that God sends to us? Their very commonness veils their blessedness. Let us seek for the good in everything. Then, though we see it not, let us never doubt that it lies hidden in every gift of God to us. Every moment brings us some benediction. Even the rough hand of trial holds in its clasp for us some treasure of love.

November 16

UNCOMMON CHRISTIANS

Be not satisfied with a mere feeble measure of spiritual life. Strive to have the abundant life and to be full-rounded Christians. Seek to have every power of your life developed to its utmost possibility of beauty and usefulness. Find out whatsoever things are pure, whatsoever things are lovely, and strive to have every mark and line of beauty in your own life. Grow toward God in all upward, heavenward reaching. Grow toward men on earth in all unselfishness and loving service. Grow in your own soul into the fulness of the stature of Christ. And all this you will gain by becoming filled more and more with Christ himself. It was the daily prayer of one saintly man, 'O God, make me an uncommon Christian.'

November 17

SELF-SACRIFICE

The path of ministry is a shining ladder steep and hard to climb, but it leads to God's feet. Whosoever would be chief, let him serve. The world is trying to scramble up another way. It thinks the path of unselfish service leads downward. But we have Christ's word that he is greatest who serves most self-forgetfully. Forget yourself. Consecrate your life to Christ. There is no other way to immortal success. Your life will seem to sink away and be lost, but it will be like the rain-drops that fall and disappear, only to come again in living beauty. No life of self-sacrifice for Christ shall fail of eternal honour.

November 18

WHAT MAKES HEAVEN?

What makes heaven? Not its jewelled walls and pearl gates and streets of golden pave and sea of glass and river of crystal, but its blessed obedience, its sweet holiness, its universal and unbroken accord with the divine will, and its spirit of love. Heaven never can be entered by any in whose hearts the spirit of heaven is not first found. Heaven must be in us, or we can never enter its gates. We are prepared for heaven, made meet for the inheritance of the saints, therefore, just in the measure in which we have learned to do God's will here on earth as it is done by angels and saints in that home of divine glory.

November 19

MISERY OF BORROWING TROUBLE

Many people are always dreading coming troubles. They are well enough now, and well enough off, but they may get sick, or they may become poor, or some other trouble may befall them. A large part of human unhappiness is caused by needless forebodings – dreading ills that never happen. It is a miserable way to live, this looking out into the future and filling it with imaginary shapes of evil. No doubt there are real troubles lying concealed in the future for all of us, but let us not dread to go on with quiet faith, since over us the bow of God's eternal goodness bends.

November 20

WHY ALWAYS PEOPLE'S FAULTS?

We are all very much alike in this world as it regards faults and failings. We all have plenty of them. Each one of us has at least enough of his own to make him very modest in pointing out those of his neighbour. The trouble is, however, that most of us have eyes so constructed or so adjusted as to see the faults of others much more clearly than our own. It is not hard to get almost anybody started at criticising others and pointing out their infirmities. What a pity it is that we have not eyes for the beautiful things in others! What a relief it would be to hear everybody you meet speaking in commendation of his neighbours and praising their virtues! Would it not be worth while to try to turn the tides of talk into this new channel for a time?

November 21

DOING IMPOSSIBLE THINGS

When God calls us to any service or task or duty whatsoever, no supposed personal incapacity, incompetency, or insufficiency may ever be urged as a reason for not obeying. God never really bids us do a thing we cannot do, and do well, with his help. He would not mock us with an unreasonable requirement. The achieving of impossible commands, of course, is not our business at all. We have nothing whatever to do with the impossible part; that belongs to God. But we have everything to do with the obeying of the command that comes to us. It is not ours to reason, to demur, to urge inability; it is ours promptly, unquestioningly to obey, and then as we go forward God will divide the water or cleave the mountain or roll away the stone. As we approach the obstacle, going in holy obedience, we shall find the way open for our feet.

November 22

BEAUTIFUL LIVING

We do not know, when we are working for immortality, by what act or word of ours we shall be remembered. It may be the obscurest thing of our life that shall shine in the most radiant glory. Let us, then, seek to make everything we do beautiful enough to be our epitaph. If our hearts are always full of love, our lives will be full of gentle deeds that will please God and bless the world. Then we shall write our names where no floods of years, no abrasion of events, no wasting tooth of decay, no hungry waves of time, eating away the bank whereon we stand, can ever destroy the record. To neglect the least duty may be to spoil our own immortality. One opportunity missed may be the marring of our whole life.

November 23

REJECTED BLESSINGS

No wonder many of us are so poor in spiritual things. To our doors evermore come the heavenly messengers, their hands laden with rich blessings which they wish to give to us. But we are so intent on our petty earthly ambitions that we do not see them nor open our doors to them; and waiting long in vain, they at last turn sadly away, leaving us unblessed in our poverty. If we would but train ourselves to take whatever gift God sends to us, we should soon become rich. God's blessings are ever at our doors. He is the giving God. The trouble with us is that we do not always recognise the blessings when they are offered to us. Some of the richest of them come in forms of pain or struggle or sorrow. Let us learn to accept God's gifts, whether they shine in joy or are veiled in shadows.

November 24

CHARACTER-QUARRIES

Every individual life has its quarries, where are hewn the blocks that are afterward built into character, where the thoughts are shaped which take form in acts and heroisms and noble works. There are two parts in every life – the heart-quarry, which the world does not see, and the life as it takes form in the eyes of men. Men must have a good heart-life before they can have a good character and make a worthy record. Men must be silent thinkers before their words or deeds can have either great beauty or wide influence. Extemporaneousness anywhere is of little value. Easy thinking never leads to very high living.

November 25

THE RADIANCE OF GOD'S WILL

There are many Christians who grieve when they cannot serve their Lord in some form of active labour for Christ. When sickness shuts them in, and they can go forth no longer to their accustomed work, they mourn that they must be so useless. They forget that that is God's will, and that the doing of God's will is always the finest thing possible in this world for any one. We worry about not carrying out our plans – the large plans we make for our own lives. But it really matters very little what comes of our plans if only we do what God marks out for us. A successful life in the end is one which has done that for which God created it.

November 26

THE CHASTENING OF LOVE

'Whom the Lord loveth he chasteneth.' So chastening is a mark of God's love, and also a seal of sonship, for he 'scourgeth every son that he receiveth'. No true father permits a child to grow up undisciplined, having its own way all the while, its life running unchecked into waywardness, wilfulness, and self-indulgence. The true father chastens. Mark, it is not punishment that God inflicts, but chastening. It is not anger or hatred that makes him at times severe, denying the child's requests. It is love that leads him to chasten. If we were not his children he would not trouble to chasten us. It is the fruitful branch the husbandman prunes to make it more fruitful; the unfruitful branch he cuts off and burns. It is the Father's child that he chastens.

November 27

REMEMBERING PAST BLESSINGS

We should remember past mercies and blessings. If we do, our past will shine down upon us like a clear sky full of stars. Such remembering will keep the gratitude ever fresh in our hearts, and the incense of praise ever burning on the altar. Such a house of memory becomes a refuge to which we may flee in trouble. When sorrows gather thickly, when trials come, when the sun goes down and every star is quenched, and there seems nothing left to our hearts in all the present, then the memory of a past full of goodness, a past in which God has never once failed us, becomes a holy refuge for our souls – a refuge gemmed and lighted by the lamps of other and brighter days.

November 28

OUR PLACE IN THE TEMPLE

The great Master-builder, in whose quarries we are now as stones that are being made ready for the temple, has a plan for his building. Every life has its own particular place in that plan. God knows what he wants you to be – how large or how small a place he wants you to fill. We must submit our lives to the hammer and the chisel and to the divine measurement, that we may be prepared for the place God is preparing for us. We must not wince under the sharp cutting of disappointment and sorrow.

'When God afflicts thee, think he hews a rugged stone
Which must be shaped, or else aside as useless thrown.'

November 29

THE BLESSING OF A BOOK

Books are not altogether impersonal things. Somebody wrote them. Somebody's life-blood is in them. Somebody lived, suffered, wept, struggled, and toiled to put into the book that which pleases and helps us. Should we not think of this as we read the sentences which delight us or which inspire and quicken us? Do we often, indeed, give thought to the writer whose written words bring to us their messages? Do we not forget ofttimes that it is somebody's heart-blood which runs in the sentences we are reading, somebody's very life, if the words are truly helpful? Do we then owe nothing to the author? Be sure the lessons he is teaching have cost him pain and tears. He had to live deeply to write helpfully. Some recognition of the help we have gotten from him we certainly owe to him. Should we not write to him our thanks for the gift he has put into our life?

November 30

THE MINISTRY OF WAITING

Each one of us does his own little part in carrying out God's great plan. If our part is to stand and wait, it is no less honourable than his who comes after us and takes up what fell from our hands and carries it on to completion. Said the blind Milton –

'They also serve who only stand and wait.'

'The world comes to him that can wait,' says the proverb; and victory comes, and rest comes, and God comes, and glory comes, to him that can wait.

DECEMBER

December 1

CLIMBING TO SAINTHOOD

Men do not fly up mountains; they go up slowly, step by step. True Christian life is always mountain-climbing. Heaven is above us, and ever keeps above us. It never gets easy to go heavenward. It is a slow and painful process to grow better. No one leaps to sainthood at a bound. Nobody gets the victory once for all over his faults and sins. It is a struggle of years, and every day must have its victories if we are ever to be final and complete overcomers. Yet while we cannot expect to reach the radiant mountain-summit at one bound, we certainly ought to be climbing at least step by step. We ought not to sit on the same little terrace, part way up the mountain, day after day. Higher and higher should be our unresting aim.

December 2

A STONE'S-CAST FURTHER

Jesus took his chosen friends with him into Gethsemane. Those who love us most truly must share our sorrow with us. But it is note-worthy, also, that Jesus himself went deeper into the shadows of the garden than he asked his friends to go. Is not this fact most suggestive? We need not fear that in any grief of ours we shall ever be alone, without companionship. We shall never find ourselves in shadows too deep for the sympathy and help of the Christ. However far into the garden of sorrow we may ever be led, if we lift up our eyes we shall see that Jesus is on before us, a stone's-cast further than he has asked us to go.

December 3

CERTAINTY OF REWARD

We need give ourselves no trouble about the reward of our life. Be it ours only to do our duty faithfully, sweetly, lovingly, all the days; then God will see that we do not miss the reward of fidelity. Our Lord suggests that the righteous will be surprised at the Judgment to learn of the glory and greatness of the services of love they have rendered to needy ones. Supposing only that they were showing kindness to the poor, they will learn that they were serving the King himself. Thus the smallest and obscurest ministry will flash out in splendid radiancy in the day of final revealing. No true service done in this world in Christ's name will fail of blessing and reward. Even the acts which seem to have been of no avail will leave a benediction somewhere. If your kind word or deed blesses no other, the doing of it will bless your own heart. Though your effort do no good to the one you meant to help, it may touch another life. Our wayside seed-sowing is not lost.

December 4

HONOURING BY TAKING

We honour God most, we make the fittest requital to him for his benefits, not by giving to him, but by receiving from him. Love wants no return for what it gives or does. God does not show favours in order to receive as much again. He gives because his heart is full of love, because he yearns to bless us. The only requital he wants is the glad acceptance of what he offers. He wants only love in return.

Consecration? Yes, but the consecration of love, and not as recompense or repayment. The Psalmist asks:

'What shall I render unto the Lord
For all his benefits toward me?'

And then he answers:

'I will take the cup of salvation,
and call upon the name of the Lord.'

December 5

HOW UNBELIEF ROBS US

Christ never compels any one to take the gifts and blessings which he has to bestow. We complain of our sparse blessedness. We wonder why God does not manifest himself to us as he has done to others. We wonder we cannot have such power in prayer as some Christians have – why so little seems to come from our work for Christ. It is not from any lack of power in Christ, for his strength never fails nor wastes; it is because we will not receive what he brings. Unbelief shuts up Christ's hand that it cannot give to us the things of his grace, or cannot work deliverances for us. Thus our unbelief keeps us impoverished. It hides God's face, and robs us of the deep, rich joys which faith would bring. Shall we not pray for simple faith, that we may receive large things?

December 6

FROZEN LOVE

There is a great deal of love that lacks affectionateness. Some one speaks of beautiful cathedrals with all their splendid architecture as 'frozen music'. There is a great deal of frozen love in this world. It is stately, strong, and beautiful, but it lacks tender expression. It lies cold and crystal in the heart, and never flows out in tenderness of word or act. There are hundreds of homes in our land in which there is love that would die for its dear ones if there were need, while yet in those very homes hearts are starving for love's daily bread.

December 7

THE BLESSING OF FRIENDSHIP

'Partners in cares' the old Romans called true friends. True friendship implies mutual helpfulness. It is not all on one side; where such friendship is there are always two shoulders under every burden. Friendship knows no limit in serving; it gives all, life itself, if need be. Its yearning is not to receive, but to give; not to be ministered unto, but to minister. The cynic sneers at the thought of friendship, but there are holy human friendships whose beauty and splendour remind us, amid the world's selfishness and hardness, that man was made in the image of God, that fragments of that image yet exist even in fallen lives, and that it is possible at last, through God's grace, to restore the heavenly lustre.

December 8

THE MISSION OF A DISCIPLE

Christ no longer goes about in person among men, laying his hands on the sick, the lame, the blind, the children. This work he has intrusted to his disciples. He wants us to represent him. He wants us to be to the sick, the sorrowing, the stricken, the fallen, what he would be to them if he were here again on the earth. It is not hard for us to know, therefore, what it is to be a true Christian. We have but to study the story of our Lord's life, watching how he helped and blessed others, to get the key to all Christian duty. His miracles we cannot repeat, but his sympathy, his gentleness, his thoughtfulness, his unselfishness, are patterns for our human imitation. If we catch his inner spirit, 'the mind that was in Christ', we will become great blessings wherever we go in his name. Then our touch will soothe, our words will comfort, strengthen, and inspire, and our deeds of love will leave benedictions on every life.

December 9

RECEIVING TO GIVE

As we receive each new lesson in life, each new piece of knowledge, each new experience, each fresh inspiration, our attitude should be one of reverent and humble unselfishness. We should say, 'This is a gift from God to me, and I am his servant. It is not mine to keep all to myself, for my own enjoyment. God gave it to me to make me more a blessing. I must not keep this light burning in the narrow chamber of my own life merely; I must place it so that it will throw its beam upon some other life.' Helen Hunt Jackson writes –

'I am a humble pensioner, myself, for my daily bread;
Shall I forget my brothers who seem in greater need?
I know not how it happened that I have more than they,
Unless God meant that I should give a larger part away.
The humblest wayside beggar and I have wants the same,
Close side by side we walked when God called out one name.
So brother, it but happened the name he called was mine;
The food was given for both – here, half of it is thine.'

December 10

UNCHRISTLIKE FORGIVENESS

There are some people whose forgiveness is little better than their malice. They never let you forget that they have forgiven you. Indeed, you sometimes almost wish they had not forgiven you at all, so miserable and so aggravating is their charity. Let us learn to forgive generously, richly, making our forgiveness complete, sweeping forever away all grudge and bitterness.

December 11

VICTORY BY WAITING

Must life be a failure for one compelled to stand still in enforced inaction and see the great throbbing tides of life go by? No; victory is then to be gotten by standing still, by quiet waiting. It is a thousand times harder to do this than it was in the active days to rush on in the columns of stirring life. It requires a grander heroism to stand and wait and not lose heart and not lose hope, to submit to the will of God, to give up work and honours to others, to be quiet, confident, and rejoicing, while the happy, busy multitude goes on and away. It is the grandest life 'having done all, to stand'.

December 12

A SURE HARVEST

While God may not give us the exact result which we hope to realize in the things we do for him, he will give some other result which will prove even better. No work for Christ will fail; no effort put forth for him will be in vain. Says Charles Kingsley –

'Not all who seem to fail have failed indeed;
What though the seed be cast by the wayside,
And the birds take it? yet the birds are fed.'

Even if there be no result here in this world, there will be a result in the world to come. Many people die and see yet no harvest from their life's sowing. But if they have been faithful, their eyes will open, when they enter heaven, on a blessed vision of ripened harvest in glory from their sowing on earth.

December 13

PROMISE AND PRAYER

There is really no true praying which is not based on a divine promise. We may never pray unqualifiedly unless there be a promise for the thing we want. But when God has promised anything to us, we can go to him with boldness and ask him to do as he has said. But why ask if he has promised? Asking shows faith. Asking is the acceptance on our part of what God offers. Ask, and ye shall receive; ask not, and ye shall not receive. Find a promise for what you want, and then bring it boldly to God. If you have no plain promise, ask humbly, submissively, and modestly, leaving altogether to his wise love the things about which you are uncertain.

December 14

'MASTER, I AM READY'

'I am ready.' That is what consecration means. It is doing what Christ commands. It is going where Christ sends you. It is not a mere devout sentiment – warmth of heart, good feeling; it is being good and doing good. Oh, be earnest. Be faithful. Be true. Be strong. Believe in Christ. Cleave to him. Do your work for him. Lift up your face toward your beloved Master's face, and say to him, 'Master, I am ready. I know not what thou hast for me to do – to work or to suffer, to live of to die – but I am ready. I am ready to speak for thee, to endure persecution for thee, to live for thee. I am ready; I am ready.'

December 15

HIS CHANGELESS LOVE

You have felt the warmth of Christ's love pouring like sunshine upon your life. You believe that he loves you today. Yet sometimes you fear for the future. 'Will his love always last?' you ask with trembling. 'May he never weary of me?' Nay; he loveth unto the end. Other things about you will fade and die; other joys will perish out of your heart; other loves will grow cold; but the love of Christ which throbs about you now will never change.

December 16

KEEP THE DOOR OF MY LIPS

No prayer should be oftener spoken by us than that of David in one of his psalms: 'Set a watch, O Lord, before my mouth; keep the door of my lips.' There is nothing in all our life to which most of us give less heed than to our words. We let them fly from our lips as the leaves fly from the trees when the autumn winds blow. Many people seem to think that words scarcely have a moral character. They watch their acts, their conduct, and then give full license to their tongues. This is not right. A true Christian should have a Christian tongue. Words have terrific power for harm if they are wrong words, and blessed, immortal power for good if they are holy words. We need to pray continually that God would keep the door of our lips and set a watch before our mouth. Only love should be permitted to interpret itself in speech. Bitterness and all evil should be restrained.

December 17

REMEMBERING KINDNESSES

At the time when help, deliverance, or favour comes to us, our hearts are very warm with grateful feeling. 'We will never forget this kindness,' we say. But do we never forget it? We remember injuries done to us. We all know how hard it is to forget a wrong that another has inflicted upon us. Sometimes we say, with martyr-like air, 'I forgive him, but I can never forget the injury.' Slights and cutting words and unkindnesses and neglects – how well we remember these! But have we as good memories for favours, kindnesses, blessings? Ought we not to have? Shall we not train ourselves rather to forget the hurts we receive as the lake forgets the ploughing of the keel through its waters, and to remember with faithful gratitude every smallest kindness done to us?

December 18

THE EXPRESSION OF LOVE

There are friendships which are true enough, but which are not hallowed by those graceful attentions and tokens of thoughtfulness which cost so little and yet are worth so much. The kindly feeling in the heart ought to find some way to utter itself – a way in keeping, too, with the delicacy and beauty of the sentiment. The affection ought to exhibit itself in amiability, in gentleness, in thoughtfulness. We ought not to be so chary of our kind words.

December 19

OUR MESSAGE TO SOULS

When you go out to seek the lost, tell them that God in heaven loves them. Tell them that his heart yearns for them as a mother's bosom yearns for her absent wandering child. No matter how sunken in sin, how depraved, how completely the divine image has been blotted from the soul, how ruined the life may be, still bend over the wreck of manhood or womanhood and whisper the blessed message, 'God loves you'. Tell it so earnestly that it cannot fail to be listened to, understood and believed. This is the message of life and hope.

December 20

FORGETTING PROMISES

A promise made to a child or to the lowliest, most unworthy person should be kept, no matter how hard it may be to keep it. 'I entirely forgot my promise,' one says, as if forgetting it were much less a sin than deliberately breaking it. We have no right to forget any promise we make to another. If we cannot trust our memory, we should make note of our promises and engagements on paper, and then keep them scrupulously, on the very minute. To break even the slightest promise is grievously to wrong and hurt another life.

December 21

NOT FAINTING UNDER TRIAL

There are some people who give up and lose all their courage and faith the moment any trouble comes. They cannot endure trial. Sorrow utterly crushes them. They think they cannot go on again. There have been lives broken down by affliction which have never risen again out of the dust. There have been mothers, happy and faithful before, who have lost one child out of their home, and have never cared for life again, letting their home grow dreary and desolate and their other children go uncared for, as they sat with folded hands in the abandonment of the uncomforted grief. There have been men with bright hopes who have suffered one defeat or loss, and have never risen again out of the dust. But God's Word teaches that we should never faint under any trial. God chastens us, not to crush us, but for our profit, that we may be partakers of his holiness. To faint, therefore, under chastening is disloyalty to God. We should accept the affliction with reverence, and turn the whole energy of our life into the channels of obedience and service.

December 22

WHAT WE SHALL BE

We have in us a life that when fully manifested will be altogether like Christ's. Christ's glory will shine in our faces; his beauty will glow in our souls. No matter how imperfect, how faulty, how full of blemishes we may be now, we are to be 'like him' when the divine life in our souls bursts out into all its richness and fulness of manifestation. With such a hope in our hearts, should we not keep ourselves from everything unworthy of such dignity and holiness, and strive to reach 'whatsoever things are lovely'?

December 23

MAKE THE LAST DAY BEAUTIFUL

The last day a friend was with us is always sacred in memory. The last walk we had together, the last talk, the last book we read, the last letter, the last goodbye, we never forget. We all want to leave sweet memories behind us in the hearts of our friends when we are gone from earth. We want our names to be fragrant in the homes on whose thresholds, in whose halls, our footfalls are wont to be heard. We can make sure of this only by so living always that any day would be a suitable and beautiful last day, leaving only tender recollections. We must make no bitterness for another life any day, because that day may be our last and that memory the one that will stay in the heart when we are gone.

December 24

O CHRIST, FORGIVE!

Oh, blessed ministry of true Christian speech! May God forgive us for the abuse or misuse of the glorious gift! If word of ours has ever hurt a tender spirit, or tarnished a white soul, or turned any away from the right path, O Christ, forgive us and help us to undo the wrong! Give us grace and wisdom, that we may use the gift of speech to honour thee and bless the world.

December 25

ON CHRIST'S BIRTHDAY

It is Christ's birthday. In among all our festivities should come sweet thoughts of the love of God. The gifts we may receive should make us think of the greatest gift of all – when God gave his Son. Let us all try to make our Christmas very full of memories of Christ. Let the blessed love of Christ make a glad Christmas in our hearts, helping us to be like Christ himself in love, unselfishness, and forgiveness.

ECHOING CHRISTMAS SONGS

What Christ is to us we ought, in our human measure, to be to others. Christmas means love. Christ came to our world to pour divine kindness on weary, needy, perishing human lives. The Christmas spirit in our hearts should send us out on the same errand. There is need everywhere for love's ministry. We should learn the true Christmas lesson of gentle, thoughtful kindness to those we love and to all we meet in life's busy ways.

December 26

CHRISTMAS LESSONS

Christmas should teach us to be Christ to others all about us, that from our very garments may flow the virtue that shall heal and bless all who touch us. There are few people whom God calls to do great things for him, but the best thing most of us can do in this world is to live out a real, simple, beautiful, strong Christian life in our allotted place. Thus in our little measure we shall repeat the life of the Master himself, showing men some feeble reflection of his sweet and loving face, and doing in our imperfect way a few of the lovely things he would do if he were here himself in our place.

December 27

DARKENED ROOMS

God carries many of his children into the darkened rooms of affliction, and when they come forth again there is more of the beauty of Christ in their souls. We get many of the best things of our lives out of suffering and pain. It may be the easiest, but it surely is not the best, life and the most blessed that is free from trial. The crown is not given to untried lives.

December 28

POWER OF FAITH

Shall we not try to learn the secret of power in Christian life and Christian work? We can do a great deal more for Christ and to bless the world than most of us are doing. It is more faith that we need. Faith links us to Christ, so that wherever we go in his name he goes with us, and whatever we do for him his power rests upon us. Every Christian life ought to be a force among men, a witness for Christ, an influence for blessing and good. Let us get nearer to Christ, that he can use us for doing the greater things.

December 29

CONSECRATION OF WILL

The highest reach of faith is loving, intelligent consecration of all our life to the will of God. We are to have desires, but they should be held in subordination to God's desires and thoughts for us. We are to have plans, but they should be laid down at God's feet, that he may either let us work them out for him or show us his plan for us instead of our own. Complete consecration of our will to God's – that is the standard of Christian living at which we are to aim. Tennyson puts this well in 'In Memoriam' –

'Our wills are ours, we know not how;
Our wills are ours, to make them thine.'

They are ours – we are sovereign in our power of will. They are to be made God's, but we must make them his; we must voluntarily yield ourselves to God. That is consecration.

December 30

HIDDEN BLESSINGS

Every hard duty that lies in your path, that you would rather not do, that it will cost you pain or struggle or sore effort to do, has a blessing in it. Not to do it, at whatever cost, is to miss the blessing. Every hard piece of road on which you see the Master's shoe-prints, and along which be bids you follow him, surely leads to a blessing, which you cannot get if you cannot go over the steep, thorny path. Every point of battle to which you come, where you must draw your sword and fight with the enemy, has in it a possible victory which will prove a rich blessing to your life. Every heavy load that you are called to lift hides in itself some strange secret of strength.

December 31

THE BLESSING OF PENITENCE

The memory of transgression will always give pain. Penitence is *not* the best thing; innocence is far better. But, having sinned, penitence is infinitely better than despair. And even out of the sin, the shame, and the sorrow God can bring blessing for ourselves and for others. While we cannot undo our wrong deeds, God can keep them from undoing us, and can even bring good out of them in some strange way, if we commit the whole matter to him.

THE END

DAILY
ENCOURAGEMENT
DAVID EVANS

'A gem in its class. It loyally fulfills the
hope kindled by its title.' J. Glyn Owen

Daily Encouragement

David Evans

People respond - and are changed – when they are encouraged.
Jesus' life was characterised by his 'ministry of encouragement'
to those he met.

Daily Encouragement is a devotional book offering the reader a
daily source of strength, support and guidance. Beginning each
day's reading with a passage from scripture, we are led through
the Bible from Genesis to Revelation. Each day's verse is
followed by a short meditation which expands on the scripture
message, challenging us to lead lives wholly dedicated to God.

David Evans has worked for Africa Evangelical Fellowship for
many years, meeting and encouraging missionaries and Christians in numerous churches.

*'...a gem in its class. It loyally fulfills the hope kindled by its
title, and that alone should be enough to recommend it in an
age when disappointment is written large across the face of
vast sections of our contemporary society.'*

**J. Glyn Owen,Minister Emeritus,
Knox Presbyterian Church, Toronto**

*'...I particularly like the way this devotional book chronologi-
cally covers the grand scope of the whole Bible. There is balance
here between essential doctrine, challenge to holy living and call
to mission.'*

Jim Pluddemann, International Director of SIM

*'Without doubt, you too will find them a means in God's hand
to encourage you in your Christian life and service.'*

Dr Geoffrey Grogan

ISBN 1- 85792-744-3

"Will encourage, challenge and stimulate you to know God better, and live in the victory made possible through his son."

Charles Price

The Life of
VICTORY

A Daily Devotional to Lift Your Spirit

Compiled by Marjorie Redpath from the works of

Alan Redpath

The Life of Victory

A Daily Devotional to Lift Your Spirit

Compiled by Marjorie Redpath from
the works of Alan Redpath

'Alan Redpath came into my life when I was a student at Moody Bible Institute in Chicago. There was an immediate heart-linking, especially together at nights of prayer. He became a great friend and supporter of Operation Mobilisation. His ministry among us was dynamic and you can get some of it in this great book!'

George Verwer, Operation Mobilisation

'The Life of Victory is vintage Redpath. Alan's heartbeat for evangelism and love for the Lord comes through in the daily readings. A year with Redpath would do any Christian good.'

**Tony Sargent,
Principal, International Christian College**

'His spoken and written ministry challenged thousands on every continent to a deeper walk with God. Now in one volume, a year long diet of daily snippets of Alan Redpath's ministry will encourage, challenge and stimulate you to know God better, and live in the victory made possible through his son.'

Charles Price, People's Church, Toronto

Alan Redpath (1907 – 1989) was the minister of Duke Street, Richmond, Charlotte Chapel, Edinburgh and Moody Church, Chicago. Once you start 'The Life of Victory' you will find yourself looking forward to putting time aside each day to meditate on what Alan has to say about how your life can be a blessing *from* God and *to* others.

ISBN 1-85792-582-3

CHRISTIAN
HERITAGE

OUR

DAILY
WALK

DAILY READINGS

F. B. Meyer

Our Daily Walk

Daily Readings

F.B. Meyer

We can all make a fresh start!

What better way than to start each day with the words of God in our minds? F.B. Meyer brings us short readings on a variety of themes to encourage, challenge and remind us of our obligations.

Our Daily Walk is a treasury of Wisdom distilled into brief and memorable reading which can be enjoyed by anyone – whether they have an hour to meditate or five minutes of peace in a hectic schedule.

'Be renewed in the Spirit of your mind'

F.B. Meyer was a very well known 19th Century Pastor and Author.

ISBN 1-85792-048-1

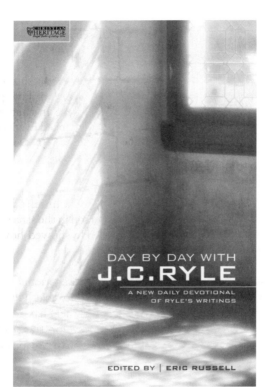

DAY BY DAY WITH
J.C.RYLE
A NEW DAILY DEVOTIONAL
OF RYLE'S WRITINGS

EDITED BY | ERIC RUSSELL

Day by Day with Ryle

A new daily devotional of J. C. Ryle's writings

Edited by Eric Russell

J.C. Ryle has become one of the most-loved of British authors on church matters. He was the first Bishop of Liverpool, managing to establish a thriving diocese in that most sectarian of English cities. Although a convinced Evangelical he was regarded as fair-minded with those who disagreed with him. Even Ryle's opponents in church politics wept when he died.

His books have remained in print for a hundred years because Ryle was able to touch the person in the street with clear teaching on doctrinal matters. He showed how the Bible was **relevant**.

His writings thus lend themselves to a devotional format and here is a new selection different to any that have gone before. Here Eric Russell (Ryle's biographer) has arranged writings according to themes that develop the reader's understanding on a topic before moving on to new pastures.

It is as refreshing as it is profound.

ISBN 1-85792-959-4

Christian Focus Publications

publishes books for all ages

Our mission statement –

STAYING FAITHFUL

In dependence upon God we seek to help make His infallible Word, the Bible, relevant. Our aim is to ensure that the Lord Jesus Christ is presented as the only hope to obtain forgiveness of sin, live a useful life and look forward to heaven with Him.

REACHING OUT

Christ's last command requires us to reach out to our world with His gospel. We seek to help fulfill that by publishing books that point people towards Jesus and help them develop a Christ-like maturity. We aim to equip all levels of readers for life, work, ministry and mission.

Books in our adult range are published in three imprints.

Christian Focus contains popular works including biographies, commentaries, basic doctrine and Christian living. Our children's books are also published in this imprint.

Mentor focuses on books written at a level suitable for Bible College and seminary students, pastors, and other serious readers. The imprint includes commentaries, doctrinal studies, examination of current issues and church history.

Christian Heritage contains classic writings from the past.

Christian Focus Publications, Ltd
Geanies House, Fearn, Tain,
Ross-shire, IV20 1TW, Scotland, United Kingdom
info@christianfocus.com

For details of our titles visit us on our website
www.christianfocus.com